ABOUT THE AUTHOR

John Langridge was educated at Marlborough College, Durham University, and the London School of Economics. He worked for multinational companies from 1989 until 2002, when he became an English teacher, having gained a CELTA (Certificate in English Language Teaching to Adults) at International House in London. He went on to teach English at two universities in France and three schools in the UK. Students from more than 70 countries attended his classes.

Much of his time was spent preparing his students for the Cambridge exams, which are now B1 Preliminary and B2 First. Unable to find grammar exercises which required words to be put into the right order in sentences - and were engaging and fun - he decided to write his own. He used these in his classes as supplementary material, helping his students put into practice the grammar they'd learnt earlier in the course. 150 texts and exercises, on a wide range of topics, are now available in his book, 'Grammar Puzzles'.

John Langridge is also the author of 'All About Us! 150 Vocabulary Exercises for school, for home, and for fun!', which was published in 2023 and is available on Amazon.

Copyright © John Langridge, 2025

The moral right of this author has been asserted.

All rights reserved.

No part of this publication may be reproduced, stored in a retrieval system, or transmitted, in any form or by any means, without the prior permission in writing of the publisher, nor be otherwise circulated in any form of binding or cover other than that in which it is published and without a similar condition including this condition being imposed on the subsequent purchaser.

Editing, design, typesetting and publishing by UK Book Publishing

www.ukbookpublishing.com

ISBN: 978-1-917329-65-1

GRAMMAR PUZZLES

CONTENTS

Introduction i
Subjects and Topics iii

Vocabulary Exercises 1

Discoveries and Inventions	2	Homes	152
English History	12	Places	162
English Literature	22	Travel	172
The Power of Speech	32	Transport	182
Politics and Government	42	Safety and Security	192
Welfare	52	Animals	202
Health and Medicine	62	Nature	212
Law and Order	72	The World	222
Words and Numbers	82	Global Problems	232
Science	92	The Weather	242
Human Beings	102	Money and Finance	252
Life	112	Food and Drink	262
Work	122	Cooking and Restaurants	272
Leisure	132	Shopping and Shops	282
Things	142	People	292

Solutions 302
Index of Topics 336

INTRODUCTION

'Grammar Puzzles' is a book of 150 texts and exercises, full of useful information and interesting facts. Every text is on a different topic and every exercise consists of five grammar puzzles.

The puzzles are made up of one or two sentences in a number of pieces, much like the pieces of a jigsaw puzzle. The challenge is to put all the pieces into the right order, so the sentences they form make sense and are grammatically correct!

All the solutions to the puzzles are on pages **302 – 335.** They're listed in alphabetical order of the titles of the texts, not numerical order, just as they are in 'All About Us!'. For example, the solutions for 1. Leonardo da Vinci are under the letter L, and those for 2. Isaac Newton, are under I. All the titles that start with the definite article 'The' are under the letter T.

English Grammar

The exercises in the book provide students with a great opportunity to put the rules of English grammar into practice. They test their understanding of the eight different parts of speech, how they're used, and the order in which they appear in a sentence. For example, a determiner in one piece of a puzzle may need to be placed in front of a noun in another piece, and a noun or a pronoun in front of a verb. A knowledge of these parts of speech, as well as adjectives, adverbs, conjunctions and prepositions, will help students decide where to put the pieces in each puzzle. Doing the exercises should improve everyone's grammar, as well as their written and spoken English, but could be particularly beneficial for native speakers of languages with word orders in sentences very different from those in English.

Facts and Information

An understanding of English grammar at intermediate level would be helpful when it comes to doing the exercises, but there is another important dimension to the book. All the texts and exercises contain interesting facts, useful information, or both. Knowing some of the facts on a wide range of subjects, including history, geography, science and nature, and having useful information about everyday life in London, the UK and the world, will all help students solve the puzzles. Reading a text and getting the gist of it before they do an exercise should also be helpful. Doing this puts everything into context, because the exercise is a continuation of the text (or precedes it) and contains facts and information on exactly the same topic. Students will already have a good idea what the exercise is about before they start the puzzles, and can use a combination of general knowledge, logic, common sense, and their understanding of English grammar, to solve them.

Teachers

The book also gives teachers an opportunity to help students improve their grammar, not only while they're doing an exercise, but also once they've finished it or done as much as they can. Writing the words from the first piece in each puzzle on the board, or putting them on a screen or a slide, is a good way of leading into the construction of the sentence (or sentences) in the puzzle. Starting there, teachers can then elicit responses from their students, asking them which piece goes next and why. The process continues until all the pieces are in the right order and the sentences have been completed.

Doing an exercise at home and finding the right sequence should be as rewarding as finishing a challenging jigsaw puzzle or putting pieces of information together to solve a mystery. It can be even more rewarding, though, for teachers and their students in a class, because of the shared sense of achievement only experienced by those working as a team.

I've taken the texts from my book of vocabulary exercises, 'All About Us!' - published in 2023 and also available on Amazon - and used them for the exercises. Some of the wording and sentences have been changed, however, so they work better as grammar puzzles.

In the years they were due to take exams, my students worked hard every week, for months, at the vocabulary and grammar exercises I gave them. Supplemented by past exam papers, these exercises greatly improved their English, and in particular, helped them do well in FCE, the Cambridge exam which is now B2 First.

'Grammar Puzzles' is intended for:

  (i)   B1 (Intermediate), and B2 (Upper Intermediate) level students, learning or revising English as a second language (ESL).
  (ii) International students doing courses in subjects other than English at universities in the UK.
  (iii) Native English speakers at school, and pupils who use English as an additional language (EAL).
  (iv) Speakers of other languages, who are learning or revising English (ESOL).
  (v)   English teachers, who can use the texts and exercises as supplementary material in their classes.

SUBJECTS AND TOPICS

Discoveries and Inventions
1. Leonardo da Vinci
2. Isaac Newton
3. Michael Faraday
4. Howard Carter
5. Alexander Fleming

English History
6. Matilda
7. Richard III
8. Henry VIII
9. Samuel Pepys
10. The Industrial Revolution

English Literature
11. Geoffrey Chaucer
12. William Shakespeare
13. Charles Dickens
14. George Orwell
15. JK Rowling

The Power of Speech
16. Emmeline Pankhurst
17. Winston Churchill
18. Martin Luther King
19. Barbara Jordan
20. Stephen Hawking

Politics and Government
21. British Politics
22. UK Political Parties
23. The European Union
24. American Politics
25. Democracies and Elections

Welfare
26. The Welfare State
27. Local Government
28. Disability
29. Care for the Elderly
30. Education, Health, and Benefits

Health and Medicine
31. Colds and Flu
32. Diseases in Poor Countries
33. Diseases in Rich Countries
34. Doctors and Chemists
35. Hospitals

Law and Order
36. Crime
37. Emergencies
38. The Police
39. The Courts
40. Punishment and Prison

Words and Numbers
41. English Grammar
42. English Vocabulary
43. Words for Feelings
44. Numbers and Calculations
45. Shapes and Sizes

Science
46. Biology
47. Chemistry
48. Physics
49. Maths
50. Computing

Human Beings
51. How We Think
52. How We Look
53. How We Move
54. How We Sound
55. Communication

Life
56. Having a Baby
57. Children
58. Growing Up
59. Adults
60. Education

Work
61. Finding Work
62. Employment
63. Interviews
64. People at Work
65. Jobs

Leisure
66. The Arts
67. Entertainment
68. Music
69. Hobbies
70. Sports and Places

Things
71. Sports Equipment
72. Tools
73. Work and School
74. Bathroom Things
75. Kitchen Things

Homes
76. Finding Accommodation
77. Houses
78. Furniture
79. Gardens
80. An Evening In

Places
81. Cities
82. The Countryside
83. Giving Directions
84. The Seaside
85. Places to Visit in London

Travel
86. Planes and Flying
87. Airports
88. Boats
89. Holidays
90. Sightseeing and Tourism

Transport
91. Learning to Drive
92. Gears and Pedals
93. Public Transport
94. Coaches and Trains
95. Safety on the Roads

Safety and Security
96. Medical Emergencies
97. Safety at Home
98. Looking after Children
99. Preventing Burglaries
100. Pedestrians and Cyclists

Animals
101. The Animal Family
102. How Animals Look
103. How Animals Move
104. How Animals Sound
105. World Records

Nature
106. Safaris, Zoos, and Farms
107. Cats and Dogs
108. Birds
109. Insects
110. Plants

The World
111. Continents and Countries
112. Oceans
113. Languages
114. World Religions
115. Earth and Other Planets

Global Problems
116. Wars
117. Poverty and Hunger
118. Disasters
119. Climate Change
120. The Environment

The Weather
121. Words for Weather
122. What Weather!
123. The Four Seasons
124. Extreme Weather
125. The Forecast

Money and Finance
126. Money and Currencies
127. Bank Accounts
128. Earning Money
129. Spending Money
130. Gambling

Food and Drink
131. Meat
132. Fish and Seafood
133. Vegetables
134. Fruit
135. Drinks

Cooking and Restaurants
136. Breakfast and Brunch
137. Lunch, Tea, and Supper
138. Cooking at Home
139. Eating in Restaurants
140. Food from Other Countries

Shopping and Shops
141. The History of Shopping
142. Shops
143. Clothes Shopping
144. Supermarkets
145. Shopping Online

People
146. What Women Wear
147. What Men Wear
148. The Body
149. The Family
150. Life and Death

GRAMMAR PUZZLES

DISCOVERIES AND INVENTIONS

1. Leonardo da Vinci

Leonardo da Vinci is known as one of the greatest artists in history. He painted the Mona Lisa, the most famous painting in the world, which hangs on a wall of the Louvre in Paris. Millions of tourists go to see the painting every year. He wasn't just an artist, though. He was also an engineer, an architect, a scientist and an inventor. Perhaps most extraordinary of all were the machines and other objects he first thought of or invented hundreds of years before anyone else. Among his inventions were flying machines, including a type of plane, a helicopter, and a parachute. He also designed tanks, a weapon similar to a machine gun, equipment for diving and swimming underwater, and a mobile bridge which moved on wheels. It's believed that he created the world's first robots as well, including one that moved like a human and another more like a car.

*Complete the text by solving the puzzles (A-E) below. The first and last pieces of each puzzle, which are in **bold**, are in the right positions, but the others aren't! Put all the pieces into the correct order and write the words on the dotted lines.*

A

He designed | than any other | and a clock that | accurate
of calculator, | was more | lenses, a type | contact | **at the time.**

....

....

B

He may | other types | how they | hurricanes and | like, and
discovered what | even have | of weather look | **move.**

....

....

C

He | there was a | as water when | same way | moved in the
invisible, | air, although | understood that | **hurricane.**

D

No-one | 500 years | pictures of the | gave us | until satellites
weather about | see this | able to | else was | **later.**

E

Leonardo | 1519, | born | was a | died in | who was | da Vinci,
in 1452 and | **genius.**

2. Isaac Newton

Isaac Newton was one of the greatest scientists in history. In 1665 he was at Cambridge University when it had to close because of a plague that had killed thousands of people in England. He returned to his mother's house in Lincolnshire and lived there for two years. There's a story that he was sitting in the garden one day under an apple tree when an apple fell on his head. However, based on what was written years later by people who knew Newton, it's more likely that he saw an apple fall from the tree straight to the ground. He told them it made him question why the apple should fall downwards and not move sideways or upwards. He then began to think that objects like the apple must be pulled towards the Earth, and in particular, the centre of the Earth. As he developed his idea, he wondered whether the force extended much further than a short distance from our planet and could even explain why the Moon goes round the Earth.

*Complete the text by solving the puzzles (A-E) below. The first and last pieces of each puzzle, which are in **bold**, are in the right positions, but the others aren't! Put all the pieces into the correct order and write the words on the dotted lines.*

A

In fact, he	objects in the	became known	the force, which
how all the	affected by	it could explain	universe are	soon realised
as gravity.				

....

....

B

Newton's	by his three	twenty	in a book	published	followed
which were	motion,	discovery was	laws of	**years later.**

....

....

DISCOVERIES AND INVENTIONS 5

C

He is also composed white light is colours of the and how
what it does, work on light, of all the famous for his **rainbow.**

....

....

D

He invented a and calculus, to do with reflect light, a type of maths
used mirrors to telescope that which is **rates of change.**

....

....

E

None helped Newton and how it about the apple, achievements,
as the story of these great well-known though, are as
discover gravity.

....

....

GRAMMAR PUZZLES

3. Michael Faraday

Michael Faraday was born in London in 1791 and was often hungry as a child because his family were poor. He left school at thirteen, worked in a bookshop and taught himself by reading books. At the age of twenty, he started attending lectures given by famous scientists, and before long he began his extraordinary career as a chemist. He discovered gases such as benzene, and found out how to turn a number of gases, including chlorine, into liquids, when no-one else thought it could be done. His work as a chemist became very important, but his contribution to physics was his greatest achievement.

Faraday was interested in magnets, which are pieces of metal that pull other metal objects towards them. He believed that magnets and electricity were related, and he became the first scientist to show that a magnet could produce electricity. Having made this discovery, he carried out experiments in which he managed to turn electrical energy into mechanical energy. In doing so, he invented and created the first electric motor. Faraday's invention has enabled us to make the machines that have become useful in so many ways in the modern world. There are cars on the roads and planes in the sky. We've got TVs, fridges and vacuum cleaners at home. Computers, mobile phones and hundreds of other machines have changed our lives.

*Complete the text by solving the puzzles (A-E) below. The first and last pieces of each puzzle, which are in **bold**, are in the right positions, but the others aren't! Put all the pieces into the correct order and write the words on the dotted lines.*

A

In 1831   energy into   process, and   experiment that   to reverse the   in another   turn mechanical   discovered   Faraday   he was able   **electrical energy.**

B

He had   a machine   very first type   dynamo, the   that produces   created the   of generator,   **electricity.**

C

Modern generators | use every | the electricity we | fossil fuels,
energy into | and renewable | now convert | nuclear power | **day.**

....

....

D

Michael | chemistry and | laws of | important | some of the
discovered | Faraday | most | **physics.**

....

....

E

His | motor and | of the electric | of the greatest | were two
inventions | the generator | **in history.**

....

....

4. Howard Carter

Lord Carnarvon was very keen on horse racing and fast cars, but he became famous around the world because of his interest in ancient Egypt. In 1914 he was given the right to dig in the Valley of Kings near the city of Luxor to find the tombs of Egyptian pharaohs. He employed an archaeologist called Howard Carter to search the area, but very little of interest or value was found and in 1922 Carnarvon decided he would only finance the search for one more season. Finally, on the 4th of November 1922, Carter and his team discovered steps, and a door that he hoped would lead to the tomb of an Egyptian pharaoh called Tutankhamun. He contacted Carnarvon and asked him to come to Egypt as soon as possible.

On the 26th of November, Carnarvon, his daughter and others watched Carter open a tiny hole in the top-left corner of the door with a chisel. He used a candle to help him look through the door into a room. "Can you see anything?" asked Carnavon. "Yes," replied Carter, "wonderful things!"

*Complete the text by solving the puzzles (A-E) below. The first and last pieces of each puzzle, which are in **bold**, are in the right positions, but the others aren't! Put all the pieces into the correct order and write the words on the dotted lines.*

A

When they   ebony   door   found   the room, they   opened the priceless gold and   and entered   **treasures.**

....

....

B

At one   door, with two   room there   of soldiers   end of the statues   was a sealed   **guarding it.**

....

....

C

This / the tomb of / room where / to another / door led / they found **Tutankhamun.**

....

....

D

It was almost / objects, many / room contained / intact, and the / in beautiful / hundreds of / in gold, or painted / of them covered **colours.**

....

....

E

They had / it was / need all his / been placed / pharaoh would / possessions in / there because / believed the young / **the afterlife.**

....

....

5. Alexander Fleming

Alexander Fleming was a doctor and researcher who worked in a laboratory in the basement of St Mary's Hospital in London. On the 28th of September 1928 he returned to work after a holiday with his family at their house in the country. He started sorting through a number of small, round dishes, sealed with lids, that he had placed in a pile before he went on holiday. The glass dishes contained a type of bacteria, tiny living things, some of which cause disease, that are visible only under a microscope. One of the dishes had been left open by mistake, and when Fleming looked at it, he noticed something very strange. A blue-green mould, a type of fungus similar to a mushroom, had grown in the dish in a circle, and destroyed the bacteria around it.

*Complete the text by solving the puzzles (A-E) below. The first and last pieces of each puzzle, which are in **bold**, are in the right positions, but the others aren't! Put all the pieces into the correct order and write the words on the dotted lines.*

A

| **If it could** | in humans and | it might be | cause disease |
| Fleming realised | in a dish, | bacteria that | kill bacteria | able to kill |
| **animals.** |

B

| **He managed** | destroyed a range of | it produced a | and discovered |
| on its own | to grow the mould | substance that | **different bacteria.** |

DISCOVERIES AND INVENTIONS 11

C

He called human body, to enough quantities, or last think it could be penicillin, but didn't the substance long enough in the produced in large **treat infection.**

....

....

D

In the of antibiotics be done, and penicillin other scientists 1940s, however, the world of medicine was one of a number showed this could that changed **forever.**

....

....

E

The substance drug that of lives became a by Fleming discovered saves millions **every year.**

....

....

ENGLISH HISTORY

6. Matilda

Matilda (who was born in 1102), was the daughter of King Henry I of England. She left England when she was still a child, and married King Henry V of Germany, who was also Holy Roman Emperor. In 1116 she travelled to Italy with her husband, and was crowned empress in a church in Rome. When Henry died in 1125, Matilda went to live in Normandy, which is in France, where she married Geoffrey of Anjou. Her father, Henry I, wanted her to rule England after him, but on his death in 1135, her cousin, Stephen, with the backing of the Church, became king. Matilda believed she had a better claim to the throne than her cousin, and in 1139, determined to do something about it, she returned to England. Supported by her half-brother, Robert of Gloucester, and her uncle, David I, king of Scotland, her army fought a civil war against Stephen's.

In the winter of 1141, Matilda was staying at Oxford Castle when it was attacked and surrounded by Stephen's army. According to a popular story of the time, she saw the snow falling heavily outside and realised enemy soldiers might not see her if she tried to escape wearing white clothes.

*Complete the text by solving the puzzles (A-E) below. The first and last pieces of each puzzle, which are in **bold**, are in the right positions, but the others aren't! Put all the pieces into the correct order and write the words on the dotted lines.*

A

When it was   accompanied   down the   white and   was lowered   of knights, she   dark, dressed in   by a number   **castle walls.**

....

....

B

Once   the frozen River   ground, she crossed   cousin's army to   straight past her   the snow-covered   she reached   Isis and walked   **safety.**

....

....

ENGLISH HISTORY

C

Although became queen much of the she never was king, while Stephen Matilda controlled of the country southwest **of England.**

D

However, when son, who became 1154, he was her cousin by Matilda's eldest died in succeeded **King Henry II.**

E

Matilda monasteries. She died worked with 1148, where she buried in Rouen the Church and founded Normandy in in 1167 and is returned to **Cathedral.**

7. Richard III

Richard III was only king of England for two years, but he is one of the most famous. This is partly because historians still can't agree whether he ordered the murder of his young nephews so that he could become king. It's also, however, because he was the last English king to die in a battle, William Shakespeare wrote a play about him, and as a result of something extraordinary that happened in 2012.

Richard was the younger brother of King Edward IV. When the king died after a short illness in April 1483, Richard was supposed to protect Edward's young sons, who were twelve and nine years old at the time. The older prince became king after his father, but his uncle may have prevented him from being crowned so he could be king instead. Richard arranged for the boys to stay in the Tower of London, a large castle next to the River Thames, but did he want them to be imprisoned and murdered, or protected? Once they were in the Tower, a law was passed by Parliament which made their parents' marriage illegal. It was claimed their father, King Edward, was already in a legal agreement to marry another woman before he married their mother. As a result of the law, the boys lost any right to the throne and Richard became the new king in July 1483.

*Complete the text by solving the puzzles (A-E) below. The first and last pieces of each puzzle, which are in **bold**, are in the right positions, but the others aren't! Put all the pieces into the correct order and write the words on the dotted lines.*

A

The young	actions made	again. Their	in public
he had arranged	and their uncle's	never seen	princes were
people think	disappearance	**their murder.**	

....

....

B

Richard and	a century	Edward III, who	were both
called Henry Tudor	from King	earlier in	a distant cousin
had died more than	descended	**1377.**	

....

....

C

Henry also believed he | the Battle of and won | August an army | had a right 1485 he led | against Richard to be king. In **Bosworth Field.**

D

Richard was killed in the | years no-one hundreds of | battle and for **buried.** | he was | knew where

E

In 2012 a found under a car park | test confirmed that skeleton was **it was Richard's.** | examined it very carefully and a DNA | in the city of Leicester. Experts

8. Henry VIII

King Henry VIII, who ruled England from 1509 to 1547, had six wives. His first wife was Catherine of Aragon, who was Spanish. After twenty-four years of marriage Henry wanted to divorce Catherine, but as a Catholic he wasn't allowed to, so he decided to change his country's religion instead. England became a Protestant country and, as a Protestant, he was able to divorce his wife. The pope in Rome was unhappy about this and punished Henry by saying he could no longer be a member of the Church.

Henry wanted to have a son to become king after him. Catherine had a baby boy but he died when he was two months old. His next wife, Anne Boleyn, gave birth to a daughter (who later became Elizabeth I), but didn't have a son. After a period of time, Henry believed Anne was seeing younger men. He became jealous and arranged for Anne to be executed. He then married Jane Seymour. She had a son (who later became the next king, Edward VI), but Jane died only two weeks after he was born.

*Complete the text by solving the puzzles (A-E) below. The first and last pieces of each puzzle, which are in **bold**, are in the right positions, but the others aren't! Put all the pieces into the correct order and write the words on the dotted lines.*

A

His fourth   a painting of   called Hans Holbein   Henry   showed   Anne of Cleves. A   famous painter   wife was   **Anne.**

....

....

B

Henry thought   when they   disappointed   but was   the painting   beautiful in   she looked   meet her,   and wanted to   **actually met.**

....

....

ENGLISH HISTORY 17

C

Although already decided   girl called Catherine   stay together
a seventeen-year-old   they didn't   he preferred   married,   they got
because he had   **Howard.**

....

....

D

Catherine became   the same fate   having sex with   before long
she suffered   accused of   his fifth wife, but   another man, and
she was also   **as Anne Boleyn.**

....

....

E

Henry's   Parr, lived   last   did. She was   than he   longer
wife, Catherine   sixth and   **lucky.**

....

....

9. Samuel Pepys

Samuel Pepys (pronounced 'peeps') was a member of parliament who also had the job of administering the English navy in the second half of the 17th century. For almost ten years between 1660 and 1669 he kept a diary, which is the main reason he is famous now. In his diary he wrote about his own personal experiences, but he also wrote about some of the great national events he witnessed, including the Great Plague. In London in 1665 about 100,000 people became ill and died because of a disease spread by fleas that lived on rats. The cause of the plague wasn't understood at the time, and a large number of dogs and cats were killed because people thought they were infected with the disease and were spreading it to human beings.

Pepys also wrote about the Great Fire of London. Early in the morning on the 2nd of September 1666 a servant woke him up to tell him about the fire, which had started at a bakery near London Bridge, and was spreading west.

*Complete the text by solving the puzzles (A-E) below. The first and last pieces of each puzzle, which are in **bold**, are in the right positions, but the others aren't! Put all the pieces into the correct order and write the words on the dotted lines.*

A

| **He** | a boat onto | a good view | London to get | the River |
| and then | Tower of | went to the | decided to take | **Thames.** |

....

....

B

| **From the** | possessions from | burning and people | see houses |
| to remove | river he could | desperately trying | **their homes.** |

....

....

C

Pepys | how serious the | king as soon | his diary that he
as he realised | went to tell the | wrote in | **situation was.**

....

....

D

It's not | disaster, but | houses were | died in the | 13,000
many people | more than | known how | **burnt down**.

....

....

E

Many | including St. | also damaged | the fire, | buildings were
historic | of London's | or destroyed in | **Paul's Cathedral.**

....

....

10. The Industrial Revolution

In Britain, for more than a hundred years after 1750, there was so much change that the period is known as the Industrial Revolution. During this period, transport and communications improved greatly. Thousands of miles of roads and canals were built, and the first railway lines began to be used in the late 1820s. People moved to the towns and cities in large numbers to work in factories. In 1750 only 15% of the population lived in towns, but by 1900 the number had risen to 85%. There were many inventions during the Industrial Revolution including photography, the bicycle, the phone and the motor car. In the early years, machines were invented for making things and better techniques were used in the factories.

*Complete the text by solving the puzzles (A-E) below. The first and last pieces of each puzzle, which are in **bold**, are in the right positions, but the others aren't! Put all the pieces into the correct order and write the words on the dotted lines.*

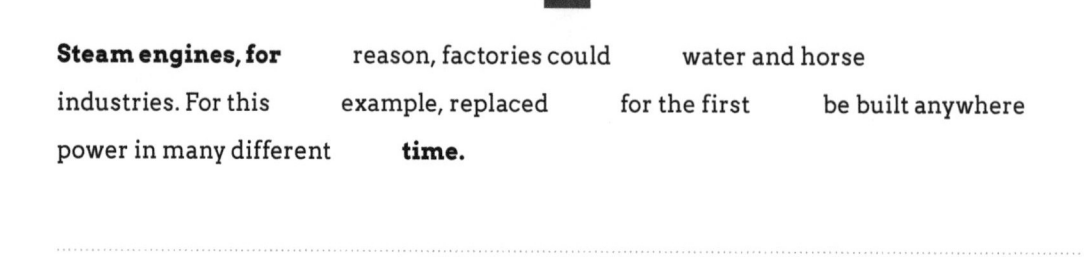

A

Steam engines, for   reason, factories could   water and horse

industries. For this   example, replaced   for the first   be built anywhere

power in many different   **time.**

....

....

B

It became   textiles, iron,   increase in   faster to produce

led to a huge   coal, which   much easier and   steel and   **production.**

....

....

C

New and farms almost production on 1700 and 1850 better ways and between also introduced of farming were **doubled.**

....

....

D

As a result became Britain changes trading a great of these **nation.**

....

....

E

There education available too. A number were important and free to the 1800s made education of laws in changes in **all children.**

....

....

ENGLISH LITERATURE

11. Geoffrey Chaucer

Known as the father of English literature, Geoffrey Chaucer was one of the greatest poets of the Middle Ages, a period in European history from the 5th to the 15th centuries. He lived from about 1343 to 1400, a time when most literature was in French or Latin, and his work helped English become accepted as an official, written language. Chaucer included approximately 2000 English words in his work that were used in spoken English, but had never been seen in written books or documents. Words we use in English, such as 'absent, accident, box, desk, finally, princess, scissors, theatre and village', all appeared for the first time in Chaucer's writings.

Chaucer had a number of different jobs during his life. He was, of course, a writer, but he was also a philosopher, an astronomer, a messenger, a soldier, an administrator, and a diplomat, who represented his country abroad. He worked for important people, including the king of England, and other people worked for him.

His life experiences must have helped him write his poetry, and in particular, his greatest work, The Canterbury Tales.

*Complete the text by solving the puzzles (A-E) below. The first and last pieces of each puzzle, which are in **bold**, are in the right positions, but the others aren't! Put all the pieces into the correct order and write the words on the dotted lines.*

A

Telling   of entertainment   14th   popular form   in the   was a   stories   **century.**

B

In The   travel together on   pilgrims tell   London to Canterbury   other as they   group of   Canterbury Tales, a   a journey from   stories to each   **Cathedral.**

C

There them are stories, most some of verse by Chaucer, but written in of which were than twenty are more **in prose.**

....

....

D

There's great the stories jobs and positions in in both the story society, and in in very different tellers, who are variety **themselves.**

....

....

E

The stories characters, who full of good amusing, and do good and are interesting, and bad **bad things.**

....

....

24 GRAMMAR PUZZLES

12. William Shakespeare

One of the greatest writers in the English language was William Shakespeare, who lived from about 1563 to 1616. During his life he wrote more than 150 sonnets, which are poems that rhyme, have fourteen lines, and ten syllables in each line. He also wrote at least 37 plays, many of which were first performed on stage by actors at the Globe and Blackfriars theatres in London. His plays, which are mainly comedies, histories and tragedies, have become so popular that they are now read and studied by millions of people, and performed in theatres all over the world.

As You Like It, Comedy of Errors, and Twelfth Night are three of Shakespeare's comedy plays. In his comedies, many of the characters make mistakes, often to do with mistaken identity, or misunderstanding what is happening. Other characters, including members of the same family, argue with each other, but in the end there's happiness and joy, with two or more people getting married.

*Complete the text by solving the puzzles (A-E) below. The first and last pieces of each puzzle, which are in **bold**, are in the right positions, but the others aren't! Put all the pieces into the correct order and write the words on the dotted lines.*

A

Shakespeare's histories　　known as the　　Richard, who　　and a civil war
16th centuries,　　Henry and　　kings called　　the 13th and　　about English
are mostly　　ruled between　　**Wars of the Roses.**

....

....

B

He　　and　　Caesar, and Antony　　Coriolanus, Julius　　plays about
wrote Roman　　also　　**Cleopatra.**

....

....

C

All of these very sad lives of real plays were unhappy endings, as many are tragedies, people in history, and stories with based on the **well as histories.**

D

This is because situations or do things characters find they have, including the main to lose everything which cause them themselves in bad **their lives.**

E

Romeo best-known Lear, are all Shakespeare's main characters in three of Hamlet, and King and Juliet, **tragedies.**

26 GRAMMAR PUZZLES

13. Charles Dickens

When Charles Dickens was still a young boy, his father lost his job and had serious problems with money. He was eventually arrested for debt and sent to prison, and before long other members of the family also left home and joined his father in prison. Dickens went to work in a factory so he could pay his rent and help his family. It was a very hard and boring job putting labels on pots ten hours a day. During this period of his life, he worked and lived in parts of London which were dirty, overcrowded, and full of poverty, rats and disease.

Dickens wrote fifteen novels between 1836 and 1870, when he died. No doubt his early experience in London helped him create the wonderful stories and characters in his books. He described in detail the city, its outskirts, the River Thames, and the places people lived and stayed in when they were travelling. He wrote about terrible working conditions, child labour in the factories, poverty, debt and crime.

Dickens' novels are full of secrets and surprises. His characters are of all ages and backgrounds: children and adults, rich and poor, good and bad.

*Complete the text by solving the puzzles (A-E) below. The first and last pieces of each puzzle, which are in **bold**, are in the right positions, but the others aren't! Put all the pieces into the correct order and write the words on the dotted lines.*

A

Some   what happens   amusing names,   relationships and   others have   are about their   very strange,   and the stories   of them are   **to them.**

....

....

B

There's   to each   not suited   who are   couples   and married   rejection,   love and   **other.**

....

....

ENGLISH LITERATURE 27

C

There are characters with younger women, husbands who who marry to wives, and others improve their social are good to their status, older men **who are not.**

D

Some are kind well and others are cruel treat children corrupt. Some are mean or and generous, others **to them.**

E

There happiness or difficult lives, Dickens' stories, normally find his characters have do bad things in but good people and many of are people who **success in the end.**

14. George Orwell

Eric Blair was a novelist and journalist who used the pen name George Orwell. At different times in his life, he was a policeman, a teacher, a soldier in the Spanish civil war, and employed by the BBC. He was born in India in 1903 but spent most of his life in England. Much of his work was influenced by his strong political views. In particular, he was opposed to totalitarian states with only one political party which had complete control and power over society. He disliked the idea that such a party should control all aspects of life, including the economy, education, and the private and public lives of its people. Orwell is best known for two novels which express these thoughts and feelings: Animal Farm, and Nineteen Eighty-Four.

In Animal Farm, which was published in 1945, pigs, horses, other animals and humans, are the main characters. It's thought it was based on the Russian Revolution, the rise of Stalin and Hitler, and a totalitarian government which eventually turns against its own people. In Nineteen Eighty-Four, he describes an unpleasant future world where the regime has total control over everything, even controlling how people think.

*Complete the text by solving the puzzles (A-E) below. The first and last pieces of each puzzle, which are in **bold**, are in the right positions, but the others aren't! Put all the pieces into the correct order and write the words on the dotted lines.*

A

Written in   become part   words and terms,   time, that have

book includes   for the first   1949, the   **of our language.**

B

Big Brother, for   Thought Police use   from those   is doing, and the

opinions different   what everyone   dictator who watches   anyone with

force to stop   example, is the   **of the regime.**

C

Orwell may / Cold War, which / expression, The / been the first / of the 20th / even have / in the second half / Union's relationship / to use the / and the Soviet / described the USA's / **century.**

D

These two / read and very / long before / wrote not / easy to / in 1950, are / he died / novels, which he / **popular.**

E

George Orwell / long word should / of his rules / using clear and / used "where a / never be / believed in / was that a / simple English. One / **short one will do".**

15. JK Rowling

JK Rowling was born in 1965 and started writing when she was six years old. One day in 1990, she was on a crowded train from Manchester to London, when she suddenly had the idea of Harry Potter, an idea that she soon developed into a story. The train had been delayed, and over a period of four hours, Rowling created the eleven-year-old boy who became the main character in seven novels that she wrote and named after him. She could picture him with black hair and glasses, an orphan who is amazed to discover he's a wizard in a world of non-magical people. The world of wizards exists in parallel with the real world, and Harry Potter goes to a school called Hogwarts to learn the magical skills he needs to succeed there. He and the other students, including his friends, Ron and Hermione, also learn how to cope with the problems faced by teenagers, such as friendship, love and hate, studying, exams and becoming adults.

*Complete the text by solving the puzzles (A-E) below. The first and last pieces of each puzzle, which are in **bold**, are in the right positions, but the others aren't! Put all the pieces into the correct order and write the words on the dotted lines.*

A

Harry Potter	wizards, and his	and wants to	powers to
killed his parents	against evil	and others	Voldemort, who
defend himself	uses his magical	main enemy, Lord	**kill him.**

....

....

B

| **The novels and** | stories | full of wonderful | on them are | films based |
| the eight | **and characters.** | | | |

....

....

C

Children enjoyed them | the world have | published | all over
book was | since the first | and adults | **in 1997.**

....

....

D

JK Rowling | name Robert | novels for | the pen | to write | went on
adults using | **Galbraith.**

....

....

E

She is best | Potter novels | other book | copies than any
known, however, | sold more | which have | for her Harry | **series.**

....

....

THE POWER OF SPEECH

16. Emmeline Pankhurst

Emmeline Pankhurst led the British suffragette movement in the early years of the 20th century. In 1903 she founded the Women's Social and Political Union with the aim of getting women the right to vote in political elections.

*Solve the puzzles (A-E) below. The first and last pieces of each puzzle, which are in **bold**, are in the right positions, but the others aren't! Put all the pieces into the correct order and write the words on the dotted lines.*

A

Although meetings were rather than words, campaigns and to direct action committed early WSPU **mainly peaceful.**

....

....

B

However, more became the suffragettes as they to be ignored, continued **militant.**

....

....

C

They opposition often became police, which and met with property, damaged from the **violent.**

....

....

THE POWER OF SPEECH

D

Many of strikes and repeatedly to were sent on hunger
when they them went were force-fed **prison.**

E

Their actions women in society experienced by and inequality
gave women the of the injustice and 1928 which raised awareness
in the law in 1918 and led to changes **right to vote.**

In November 1913, Pankhurst gave a speech to an audience in the US which included these words:

"It has come to a battle between the women and the government…Now, I want to say to you who think women cannot succeed, we have brought the government of England to this position, that it has to face this alternative: either women are to be killed or women are to have the vote. I ask American men in this meeting, what would you say if…you were faced with that alternative, that you must either kill them or give them their citizenship? Well, there is only one answer…you must give those women the vote…I come to ask you to help win this fight. If we win it, this hardest of all fights, then, to be sure, in the future it is going to be made easier for women all over the world to win their fight when their time comes."

17. Winston Churchill

When Winston Churchill became British prime minister and leader of a wartime coalition government on the 10th of May 1940, his appointment was unpopular with many MPs.

*Solve the puzzles (A-E) below. The first and last pieces of each puzzle, which are in **bold**, are in the right positions, but the others aren't! Put all the pieces into the correct order and write the words on the dotted lines.*

A

During the politicians the House of Commons respect of summer of 1940, the support and of speeches in made a number which won him however, he **of all parties.**

....

....

B

The British affected by his in the US and across radio also deeply the world, were public, and millions **broadcasts.**

....

....

C

They gave at a very itself against dangerous and would defend hope that Britain Adolf Hitler people belief and **difficult time.**

....

....

D

When he and 'fight', great effect, none (taking action to stop (winning the war), number of words to more so than 'victory', spoke, he repeated a **the enemy).**

E

Churchill's forces to carry ended armed the Second World War encouraged its a nation, and inspired on fighting until speeches **in 1945.**

"I have nothing to offer but blood, toil, tears, and sweat," he said on 13th May. "You ask, what is our aim? I can answer in one word: victory. Victory at all costs – victory in spite of all terror – victory, however long and hard the road may be, for without victory there is no survival." Then, on the 4th of June, just before the Battle of Britain, he spoke again in the House of Commons. "We shall go on to the end, we shall fight in France, we shall fight on the seas and oceans, we shall fight with growing confidence and growing strength in the air, we shall defend our island, whatever the cost may be, we shall fight on the beaches, we shall fight on the landing grounds, we shall fight in the fields and in the streets, we shall fight in the hills; we shall never surrender..." On the 20th of August, as British air force pilots were fighting in the air above Britain, Churchill spoke about the importance of their actions. "The gratitude of every home in our island...goes out to the British airmen who...are turning the tide of the World War...Never in the field of human conflict was so much owed by so many to so few."

36 GRAMMAR PUZZLES

18. Martin Luther King

Martin Luther King Junior led the civil rights movement in the US in the 1950s and 60s. He was committed to nonviolent action and resistance, having been inspired by Mahatma Gandhi, and his own Christian beliefs as a Baptist minister. A civil rights activist, he organised and led campaigns for racial equality on behalf of African Americans, before going on to campaign against poverty and the Vietnam War. He was imprisoned many times, but his work raised awareness of inequality and injustice across the world.

*Solve the puzzles (A-E) below. The first and last pieces of each puzzle, which are in **bold**, are in the right positions, but the others aren't! Put all the pieces into the correct order and write the words on the dotted lines.*

A

It also   law which   in US   changes   ended legal   led to   **segregation.**

....

....

B

In 1964, aged   Prize for   man to   win the Nobel   became the   35, he   youngest   **Peace.**

....

....

C

Despite   1968 he was   Memphis,   danger, and in   was often in   by a gunman in   this, his life   assassinated   **Tennessee.**

....

....

D

In the holiday in his Monday every a national US, the third January is **honour.**

....

....

E

Schools, public towns have than 700 streets buildings been named in cities and and more **after him.**

....

....

In 1963, Martin Luther King, and others, organised and led a march on Washington for jobs and freedom. At the Lincoln memorial, in front of more than 200,000 people, he gave one of the greatest speeches of all time. Known as "I Have a Dream", it was seventeen minutes long, and included these words:

"I say to you today, my friends, so even though we face the difficulties of today and tomorrow. I still have a dream. It is a dream deeply rooted in the American dream. I have a dream that one day this nation will rise up and live out the true meaning of its creed. We hold these truths to be self-evident that all men are created equal. I have a dream that one day, on the red hills of Georgia, the sons of former slaves and the sons of former slave owners will be able to sit down together at the table of brotherhood… I have a dream that my four little children will one day live in a nation where they will not be judged by the colour of their skin, but by the content of their character. I have a dream today."

19. Barbara Jordan

*Solve the puzzles (A-E) below. The first and last pieces of each puzzle, which are in **bold**, are in the right positions, but the others aren't! Put all the pieces into the correct order and write the words on the dotted lines.*

A

Barbara rights politician, and a the civil a lawyer, Democratic leader of Jordan was **movement.**

....

....

B

In 1966 she first African American to win a seat Senate since Senate, and the black woman member of the in the Texas became the first **1883.**

....

....

C

In 1972 she was Representatives in her Congress, the first House of elected to Texas in the woman to represent **own right.**

....

....

D

She though, for political known, two important is best **speeches.**

....

....

E

In 1974 she supporting president, Richard speech of the American televised made a the impeachment **Nixon.**

....

....

Two years later, she became the first African American woman to make the keynote speech at a Democratic National Convention, which included these words:

"We believe in equality for all and privileges for none...This is a belief that each American, regardless of background, has equal standing in the public forum. All of us. Because we believe this idea so firmly, we are an inclusive rather than an exclusive party...We believe that the government, which represents the authority of all the people, not just one interest group, but all the people, has an obligation actively to seek to remove those obstacles which would block individual achievement; obstacles emanating from race, sex, economic condition. The government must seek to remove them. We are a party of innovation. We do not reject our traditions, but are willing to adapt to changing circumstances, when change we must. We are willing to suffer the discomfort of change in order to achieve a better future. We have a positive vision of the future, founded on the belief that the gap between the promise and reality of America can one day finally be closed. We believe that."

20. Stephen Hawking

*Solve the puzzles (A-E) below. The first and last pieces of each puzzle, which are in **bold**, are in the right positions, but the others aren't! Put all the pieces into the correct order and write the words on the dotted lines.*

A

Stephen Hawking, 2018, author and born in who was was a physicist, died in 1942 and **researcher.**

....

....

B

He is best of the work on the for his development known origins and **universe.**

....

....

C

He suffered cosmologist, and work as a his life, but in disabled he continued to model for illness for most of a spokesperson and role spite of this from a serious **people.**

....

....

D

He and signed a human and civil rights for the world's charter on disability in 2000 which demanded 600 million eleven others **disabled people.**

E

He was lectures and interviews on involved activities and gave numerous talks, in many fundraising **disability.**

On the 29th of August 2012 at the opening ceremony of the Paralympic Games, he communicated these words to a worldwide audience:

"The Paralympic Games is also about transforming the perceptions of the world. We are all different. There is no such thing as a standard or run of the mill human being – but we share the same human spirit. What is important is that we have the ability to create. This creativity can take many forms – from physical achievements to theoretical physics. However difficult life may seem, there is always something you can do and succeed at." Soon afterwards, in September 2012, his interview with the BBC included these words: "People have come to realise that the disabled are normal people who just happen to have certain special difficulties... I believe science should do everything possible to prevent or cure disability. No-one wants to be disabled if it can be avoided. I was diagnosed with motor neurone disease at the age of 21... That I'm still alive at the age of 70 is due in large part to the excellent care I have received. It has also helped that I have been successful in my scientific career. This has kept me active and I travel a lot although I'm almost paralysed. I hope my example will give encouragement and hope to others in similar situations. Never give up."

POLITICS AND GOVERNMENT

21. British Politics

The United Kingdom, known as the UK, is a democracy and a monarchy, and a monarch (a king or a queen), is the head of state. The prime minister is the head of government and leader of the political party which has won a general election. After the election, he or she chooses about twenty members of parliament, or MPs, from the party to become members of a powerful group called the Cabinet. Each of these senior politicians is in charge of a department. There are departments for every important area of government, including the economy, education, health, the environment, and transport.

In a general election, normally held every five years, candidates from different parties compete against each other to win a seat in the House of Commons and become an MP.

*Complete the text by solving the puzzles (A-E) below. The first and last pieces of each puzzle, which are in **bold**, are in the right positions, but the others aren't! Put all the pieces into the correct order and write the words on the dotted lines.*

A

To do | than any other | or her local | called a | more votes | candidate in his | has to get | area, which is | this, a candidate | **constituency.**

....

....

B

Once | constituency in | the people in | new MP | his or her | represents all | elected, the | **Parliament.**

....

....

C

A party | a majority of | become the | 650 seats, to win | than half of the
has to have | the election and | MPs, or more | **government.**

....

....

D

If no party | gain a small | seats try to | with the most | the parties
to do this, | manages | **majority.**

....

....

E

This is done | other parties, so | is more | one of the | seats, or MPs,
coalition with | number of | by forming a | their combined | **than 325.**

....

....

22. UK Political Parties

Since the 1920s, the two largest political parties in the UK have been the Conservatives and Labour. The Conservatives are sometimes called the Tory party and their members and supporters are known as Tories. Their policies used to be considered right-wing, but are now often described as centre-right. They've tried to lower taxes and reduce public spending by making cuts to public services in the UK, which has included local government, health care and transport. Another priority has been to reduce the national debt, which is billions of pounds.

The Labour Party historically has been a left-wing party – now considered by many to be centre-left – which has normally supported higher taxes and increased public spending. They've accused the Conservatives of helping rich people in the Southeast and not doing enough to help poorer people in other parts of the country. When Labour won the general election with a large majority in 2024, they promised to help everyone.

*Complete the text by solving the puzzles (A-E) below. The first and last pieces of each puzzle, which are in **bold**, are in the right positions, but the others aren't! Put all the pieces into the correct order and write the words on the dotted lines.*

A

In particular, they   bills by using   health service   crime, reform the   cut household   halve violent   create jobs,   and education system, and said they would   **cheaper electricity.**

....

....

B

In recent   Commons than   in the House of   Conservatives and parties - after the   won more seats   have been three   decades, there Labour – that have   **the others.**

....

....

C

These are the Party and the of Northern Nationalist Unionist Party the SNP, or Scottish Liberal Democrats, DUP, or Democratic **Ireland.**

D

In 2010 the order to form join them in asked the DUP, to and in 2017 they the Liberal Democrats, a coalition Conservatives asked **government.**

E

The Conservatives and become to gain a small needed their MPs House of Commons of seats in the majority **the government.**

46 GRAMMAR PUZZLES

23. The European Union

The European Union, known as the EU, is an economic and political union of 27 member states. It operates through a system of independent organisations, such as the European Parliament and the European Central Bank. It also operates with the help of European governments whose politicians have meetings, talk to each other and make decisions. As a result, the EU has developed a single market, and makes laws for all its member states. Some of these laws ensure the free movement of people, goods, services and money across borders in the EU. Others make it possible for countries to work together on crime and immigration and have common policies on trade, agriculture, fisheries and regional development. Regional development is intended to help countries do better business, improve their economies and create jobs. Climate change, energy supply and globalisation are all part of the policy too. Globalisation is to do with countries becoming more similar and connected to each other because of large international companies and the Internet.

*Complete the text by solving the puzzles (A-E) below. The first and last pieces of each puzzle, which are in **bold**, are in the right positions, but the others aren't! Put all the pieces into the correct order and write the words on the dotted lines.*

A

Most   use their own   euro, although   have the same   some countries   currency, the   EU countries   **currency.**

....

....

B

The European   keeping inflation   policies for the   Germany, has   particular,   Frankfurt,   euro, and in   Central Bank in   **under control.**

....

....

POLITICS AND GOVERNMENT 47

C

This means of everything go up too sure the price doesn't making in the shops **quickly.**

D

The UK joined 2016, after 43 years should remain the 23rd of June whether the UK 1973. On held to decide the EU in referendum was of membership, a **in the EU.**

E

52% of people a member of to remain. In a ceased to be Brexit, the UK known as to leave, and 48% came to be who voted chose process that **the EU.**

24. American Politics

The United States of America is a republic with a federal government. This means that each of the fifty states has control over its own political activities, but whenever national decisions are made, the states are controlled by central government in Washington DC. The constitution of the US divides the federal government into three branches to make sure no individual or group has too much power. These branches are the Legislature (Congress), which makes the laws; the Executive (the President, Vice President and the Cabinet), which ensures the laws are carried out or actioned; and the Judiciary (the judges of the Supreme Court and the federal courts). The President, who's in charge of the Executive (but isn't a member of Congress), is supposed to be advised by the Cabinet, which includes the heads of the executive departments and other senior government officials. Congress consists of the Senate and the House of Representatives, known as the House. The Senate is smaller than the House (there are two senators for every US state), but its members are more senior and include the Vice President. In the House, the number of representatives from each state is related to the size of its population.

*Complete the text by solving the puzzles (A-E) below. The first and last pieces of each puzzle, which are in **bold**, are in the right positions, but the others aren't! Put all the pieces into the correct order and write the words on the dotted lines.*

A

California has representatives, which have only one largest number of the smallest populations also has the than fifty. States with population, so it the largest can be more **representative.**

....

....

B

In total, there or Republican and 435 representatives are either Democrat are 100 senators in Congress, who **politicians.**

....

....

POLITICS AND GOVERNMENT 49

C

Democrats, who tend to be more left-wing, normally support higher taxes, and more money for public services such as health **care and education.**

D

Republicans tend to be more right-wing and believe in the right to possess guns, and the death **penalty.**

E

Their policies usually result in lower taxes, but less money for public services and increased military **spending.**

25. Democracies and Elections

One of the best things about democracies is that people can choose and vote for the politicians they want in an election. We're very lucky not to live in a country ruled by a dictator, or where there is only one political party. Dictators believe they can do whatever they want. This includes using force against their own people, especially if there are protests or demonstrations against the dictator. Democracies are not perfect, but most people agree they're a better form of government than any alternative.

Before an election, opinion polls give people an idea of how popular the parties are. Each party tries to get as much publicity as possible so that the voters learn more about the party's candidates and their policies. Senior politicians and other party members travel round the country, going from door to door, meeting people and making speeches. There are party political broadcasts and adverts online and in newspapers. Party leaders take part in debates on television.

*Complete the text by solving the puzzles (A-E) below. The first and last pieces of each puzzle, which are in **bold**, are in the right positions, but the others aren't! Put all the pieces into the correct order and write the words on the dotted lines.*

A

On people station to constituency, local polling in each polling day, go to their **vote.**

....

....

B

They are and their parties has the names candidates paper which a piece of given of the local **on it.**

....

....

C

They put a wish to · the name of · and party they · cross next to the person · **vote for.**

....

....

D

Then they container · paper in a · called · piece of · put their **a ballot box.**

....

....

E

At the parliament for · the candidate with · counted and · member of votes are · becomes the · day, all the · end of the · the most votes **their local area.**

....

....

WELFARE

26. The Welfare State

A welfare state is a country whose government makes sure its people receive the practical and financial help they need. In a welfare state there is less poverty than in countries without welfare. People have more opportunities and a fairer share of a country's wealth. Those earning a lot of money pay more tax than others who don't earn very much. People with no income, or very low incomes, pay no tax. In the UK, the money raised by these taxes goes towards the pensions and benefits that are given to people in need. They also pay for services such as health, which is provided by the National Health Service, and care and education, provided by local government.

*Complete the text by solving the puzzles (A-E) below. The first and last pieces of each puzzle, which are in **bold**, are in the right positions, but the others aren't! Put all the pieces into the correct order and write the words on the dotted lines.*

A

The welfare | young and elderly | and 1914, when | people who | reforms to help | UK was created | there were | state in the | between 1906 | **were poor.**

....

....

B

Free school | too old to | financial support | there was | children, and | given to | were sick, or | medicals were | meals and | for adults who | **work.**

....

....

C

This was Beveridge, an and social report, named later in 1942, economist after William followed, years by the Beveridge **reformer.**

D

The report people in care, education, government to employment for advised the income, health housing and provide enough **need.**

E

By 1948 new had asked financial help resulted the Beveridge report introduced which in the practical and laws had been **for.**

54 GRAMMAR PUZZLES

27. Local Government

In the UK, the national government is responsible for running the country. Local government deals with towns, the areas around them, and parts of cities. In London there are 32 local governments which are called councils. The income tax that people pay goes to the national government who then give some of it to the councils. There is a separate tax, called council tax, that people pay directly to their local council, which also pays for local services. The amount of council tax paid is related to the value of each person's home, so people who own expensive properties pay more than people who own cheaper ones. Once they receive the money, councils spend it on different services intended to help local people and their families in their everyday lives.

*Complete the text by solving the puzzles (A-E) below. The first and last pieces of each puzzle, which are in **bold**, are in the right positions, but the others aren't! Put all the pieces into the correct order and write the words on the dotted lines.*

A

The services   housing, waste and   transport, leisure,   include education,
local government   provided by   that are   **social services.**

B

Social   support of disabled   and adults at   for the care and
are responsible   as children   services departments   people, as well
and elderly   **risk.**

C

There are services and parking, roads, by councils other services libraries, the emergency too, such as provided **planning.**

....

....

D

Planning change a building an extension, or example, to departments deal window, build door or a replace a with applications, for **into flats.**

....

....

E

The National almost everything councils, but Service, or NHS, by local is not provided Health **else is.**

....

....

28. Disability

Disability is a word used to describe a physical or a mental impairment that may prevent some people from doing things other people are able to do. For many disabled people, it's caused by a part of the body which doesn't function. Other disabled people have lost a part of the body in an accident, a war or because of a disease. Disability can be inherited, happen during birth or while growing, or be caused by illness or injury.

The challenge for a caring society is to enable people with disabilities to live as full a life as possible. With modern technology it is now possible to do far more than it was hundreds of years ago. Wheelchairs and artificial limbs were in use by 1800, but they are now widely available and can improve the lives of more people with disabilities than ever before. Another important development has been a wide range of computer software which has made it easier for disabled people to communicate, work and socialise.

*Complete the text by solving the puzzles (A-E) below. The first and last pieces of each puzzle, which are in **bold**, are in the right positions, but the others aren't! Put all the pieces into the correct order and write the words on the dotted lines.*

A

In 1948 injured UK began hospital in the to help doctors at a using sport **soldiers.**

....

....

B

Since and psychological lives because important been an people's then, sport has of its physical part of disabled **benefits.**

....

....

C

Millions of part disabilities every in sports take athletes with **day.**

....

....

D

Many have like the events Games and the Invictus in sports the Paralympic competed Special Olympics, **Games.**

....

....

E

Disabled what can life, are people in the world showing sport, and in **be achieved.**

....

....

29. Care for the Elderly

Although many people continue to be active, happy and well in later life, old age increases the chance of longer-term medical conditions and problems. Elderly people are more likely to suffer from frailty, dementia, disability, illness, and dependence. Much can be done for many of these people to enable them to carry on living at home and being independent, and in some cases elderly people are cared for and looked after by a member of the family. Other people, however, move into care homes when it is no longer safe for them to live at home, they can no longer look after themselves, or they choose to do so.

In the UK, charities and the social services departments of local councils also offer a range of services. These make it possible for people to continue living in their own homes, and special equipment such as stairlifts can be installed in their houses. There are carers who help elderly people get up in the morning, wash and get dressed. They visit some of them during the day and help them go to bed in the evening. Many also do the shopping for people who are unable to do it themselves. Others make sure elderly people have hot meals brought to their homes when they have stopped cooking for themselves.

*Complete the text by solving the puzzles (A-E) below. The first and last pieces of each puzzle, which are in **bold**, are in the right positions, but the others aren't! Put all the pieces into the correct order and write the words on the dotted lines.*

A

Loneliness   elderly   for   problem   is a   many   **people.**

....

....

B

They feel   see, or spend   knew when they   no longer   alone and people they   they live   because   lonely   time with, the **were younger.**

....

....

C

Charities and part in daytime | groups and take help by | them to join try to | arranging for councils | **activities.**

....

....

D

Much more neighbours to deal | and members of with the **the family.** | situation, including could be | done, however, visits from | more regular

....

....

E

The challenge society is to make not on their | own, live as receive the **need.** | people are possible, and | care they full a life as | sure elderly for a caring

....

....

60 GRAMMAR PUZZLES

30. Education, Health, and Benefits

In a welfare state, taxes are paid to a government and the government uses the money to pay for services and benefits. Two of the main services are education and health care.

There are private schools in the UK, but most schools are state schools. Private schools can be very expensive, but state schools are free, which means parents don't have to pay for their children's education. There are private hospitals in the UK, too, but the National Health Service, or the NHS as it is known, provides free health care for everyone who needs treatment. Someone with a medical problem can go to see a doctor who is called a GP (short for general practitioner), and they don't have to pay for the service. If someone needs to go to hospital and stay there for a period of time, this is free as well.

*Complete the text by solving the puzzles (A-E) below. The first and last pieces of each puzzle, which are in **bold**, are in the right positions, but the others aren't! Put all the pieces into the correct order and write the words on the dotted lines.*

A

| **There are also** | government for | need financial | by the | provided |
| are payments | people who | benefits, which | **help.** | |

B

For people	age there's a state	benefit. For men	find a job
reached retirement	who have	work and can't	who are out of
and women	there's unemployment	**pension.**	

C

There are after other people, too, for disabled payments carers who look and for **people.**

D

Income to pay their low incomes people on benefit helps incomes, and housing people on low support is for **rent.**

E

Many of the benefit, an adoption children. There's maternity related to other benefits are incomes there's child families on low payment, and for **benefit.**

HEALTH AND MEDICINE

31. Colds and Flu

When you're working or studying it's important that you feel well so you can do your best. There are some very common illnesses that affect more of us in the winter than at other times of year. If you get a cold (you can also say catch a cold), you'll have a number of symptoms. A cold often starts in your head and makes you feel tired and unwell. A day or two later the cold normally spreads to your nose and throat, before it moves to your chest. You'll probably need some tissues to wipe your nose. You may sneeze a lot and have a sore throat. Colds tend to last a few days or a week, but some can last for months. This is because they're caused by more than 200 viruses and some of these make us ill for longer than others.

*Complete the text by solving the puzzles (A-E) below. The first and last pieces of each puzzle, which are in **bold**, are in the right positions, but the others aren't! Put all the pieces into the correct order and write the words on the dotted lines.*

A

You don't   if they don't   normal lives even   on with their   cold. Most

to stay in bed   usually have   people carry   if you have a

feel very well.

....

....

B

If you get   won't feel able   probably feel   work during   though, you'll

(or catch) flu,   to study or   much worse and   **the day.**

....

....

C

With flu, you could have a which is when you when your temperature rises, or chills, headache or a fever, which is **feel very cold.**

D

You may symptoms I've some or all times. You'll of the cold cold at different feel hot and also have **mentioned.**

E

Both colds bed and rest sensible thing to people. If you have try not to go and flu are until you feel do is to go to flu, the most near other very infectious so **better.**

32. Diseases in Poor Countries

There are many diseases in the world that are related to poverty. People are still very poor in some countries. As a result, they suffer from malnutrition. They become ill because they don't have enough food to eat, or are eating the wrong food. In many cases they don't have clean water either. Clean water is needed for people to drink. It's needed when people wash themselves, too, and when they wash their clothes. It's also needed for cooking. Without it, diseases spread quickly, especially in crowded, dirty living conditions.

In parts of Africa, there are three very serious diseases which kill people every day: malaria, tuberculosis, or TB, and HIV AIDS. In these places there isn't enough health education or health care. This means people don't know about the dangers or can't avoid them. What makes everything worse is that most of them won't get the right medical help when they're sick.

*Complete the text by solving the puzzles (A-E) below. The first and last pieces of each puzzle, which are in **bold**, are in the right positions, but the others aren't! Put all the pieces into the correct order and write the words on the dotted lines.*

A

It's common   the same   and HIV at   malaria   have both
for people to   **time.**

....

....

B

When this   stronger, so   other people   HIV virus   happens, their
they infect   is much   **more easily.**

....

....

C

People with systems are with TB. This is from malnutrition, can HIV, or who suffer because their immune become ill **low.**

D

In Africa, more anything of TB than because their lives HIV lose people with **else.**

E

If there's children are likely to place, more die. It's a tragic all in one water, and disease malnutrition, dirty become sick and men, women and **situation.**

33. Diseases in Rich Countries

Many of the diseases people suffer from in rich countries are related to how we live. We choose a particular lifestyle because we enjoy it and can afford it. It's easy and fun to drive everywhere, so we stop walking. We've got TVs, computers and mobile phones, so we spend our evenings and weekends at home instead of going out. During the week many of us go to school, or work, and sit at a desk all day. There's less time to take exercise.

We can choose what we like to eat or drink, but so much of what we choose is bad for us. Food with a lot of fat in it, or sugar, or both. We put salt in our cooking and on our plates. We don't eat enough fruit and vegetables. Many of us still smoke cigarettes as well, and we drink too much alcohol. It's a lifestyle that can cause problems later in life. A lack of exercise, poor diet, being overweight, smoking, and drinking, can all result in a number of serious illnesses. One of the most serious is cancer.

*Complete the text by solving the puzzles (A-E) below. The first and last pieces of each puzzle, which are in **bold**, are in the right positions, but the others aren't! Put all the pieces into the correct order and write the words on the dotted lines.*

A

There   organs in, the   cancer, which   parts of, or   affect different   types of   are many   **body.**

B

Some forms   diagnosed   they are   people still   cured, but   can be   of the illness   forms unless   die of other   **early.**

C

Other serious illnesses are heart strokes. People of dying from heart with heart disease are in danger disease and **attacks.**

D

If someone has there's bleeding, and the brain becomes blocked, or this can also be a stroke, a blood vessel in **fatal.**

E

It's not likely to change our all bad die of these much less news, though. We're **lifestyles!** illnesses if we

34. Doctors and Chemists

If you're not feeling well, or you've got an ache in a part of your body, what do you do? If you don't think it's serious, you could go to your local chemist and get something to treat it. The chemist, who sells medicines (and almost anything you might need in your bathroom), may be able to help, but if not, they normally advise you to see a doctor. There should be a surgery near you where there are doctors who can examine you to see what the problem is. You will need to contact the surgery and register with them. Once you've registered you can ask for an appointment. When you go to your appointment, which may be a few days or weeks later, the doctor will diagnose the problem and help you get the right treatment.

*Complete the text by solving the puzzles (A-E) below. The first and last pieces of each puzzle, which are in **bold**, are in the right positions, but the others aren't! Put all the pieces into the correct order and write the words on the dotted lines.*

A

If it's a	chemist and	treat, they	tablets	back to your	is easy to
or some	you to go	problem which	buy a cream,	may tell	
over the counter.					

....

....

B

| **But if you** | doctor will | for it, which is | medicine, the | need a strong |
| sent to the | prescription | give you a | **chemist.** | |

....

....

C

Once for you to you it's ready text telling should receive a by the chemist, you prepared has been the medicine **collect.**

....

....

D

Your doctor referred to see problem is, in normally be your medical you would sure what which case may not be **a specialist.**

....

....

E

This doctor with a you to see a illness that you're body or the arrange for part of the knowledge of the means they lot of medical **worried about.**

....

....

35. Hospitals

In the UK, when someone has an accident and gets injured, or feels very sick, they may have to call 999 and ask for an ambulance to take them to hospital. The ambulance reaches them as soon as it can, and a paramedic might have to give the casualty some medical treatment before they set off. If they don't need an ambulance, most people who are injured or sick are driven to hospital by a friend or relative or take themselves. When they arrive, they go to the A&E department which stands for Accident and Emergency. They wait there for their turn to see a doctor who decides what treatment is needed. People who have treatment and go home the same day are known as outpatients. Other people who stay in hospital overnight or for several days or weeks are called inpatients.

*Complete the text by solving the puzzles (A-E) below. The first and last pieces of each puzzle, which are in **bold**, are in the right positions, but the others aren't! Put all the pieces into the correct order and write the words on the dotted lines.*

A

Hospitals have   cuts, cancer and   types   as burns and   for different   sickness, such   of departments   a number   of injury or   **heart disease.**

....

....

B

There's   an intensive care   very serious   department as   normally a maternity   or illnesses there's   well, and for   injuries   **unit.**

....

....

C

Most departments have are beds in wards and there rooms called each ward for **inpatients.**

D

People who insurance may have private have medical normally choose to go to a bedroom and can a private **hospital.**

E

In the NHS, or National Health Service, and hospitals are part of the UK, however, most large are public **hospitals.**

LAW AND ORDER

36. Crime

If someone does something wrong and breaks the law, we say a crime has been committed. Different words are used in the English language for different crimes and the people who commit them. A murderer commits a murder and a rapist is guilty of rape. Terrorists cause terrorism and hijackers hijack planes or cars. Muggers mug people, burglars burgle houses and robbers rob shops, post offices or banks. Arsonists commit arson. For people who lose their lives or suffer physical or psychological harm as a result of serious crimes, and for their families, these are terrible events. Most of us, however, only find out about the worst offences when they're reported in the news, because as terrible as they are, they are still relatively infrequent.

There are other crimes that are more common, though. Do whatever you can to avoid becoming the victim of a crime. When you're in the street make sure any valuables you're carrying, such as money and mobile phones, are hidden from view and can't be stolen from your bag.

*Complete the text by solving the puzzles (A-E) below. The first and last pieces of each puzzle, which are in **bold**, are in the right positions, but the others aren't! Put all the pieces into the correct order and write the words on the dotted lines.*

A

Be very | or pin | financial | any passwords | personal or
banking and | careful with | information, online | **numbers.**

....

....

B

Don't buy | buying and they | can never be | dealer. You | ill or even kill
a drug | drugs from | could make you | sure what you're | **you.**

....

....

LAW AND ORDER 73

C

Never get | much more | alcohol or taking | with a driver | a car accident
into a car | likely to be in | drugs. You're | who's been drinking | **if you do.**

....

....

D

If you're | a cyclist, look | pedestrian, or | drivers | driving, or a
dangerous | out for | **too.**

....

....

E

Dangerous | are careless or drive | motorists | our roads every
and people die on | driving is a crime | day because | **too fast.**

....

....

37. Emergencies

An accident or a crime can become an emergency. In an emergency someone who witnesses what's happened calls the emergency services by dialling 999 and asks for the ambulance, the fire service, or the police. In a situation where one of the emergency services needed is the police, police officers on foot or in police cars go as fast as possible to the scene of the incident. If someone has been injured, an ambulance drives to the scene and a fire engine may go to put out a fire. These vehicles all have sirens and flashing lights so people can hear them, see them, and move out of their way to let them go past.

When the emergency services arrive, they often find people who are upset, angry, or frightened. Anyone who is hurt or injured is usually treated in the ambulance by a paramedic and taken to hospital. If the police think someone may have caused an accident or committed a crime, they talk to the people involved, and any witnesses, asking questions about what they saw or did.

*Complete the text by solving the puzzles (A-E) below. The first and last pieces of each puzzle, which are in **bold**, are in the right positions, but the others aren't! Put all the pieces into the correct order and write the words on the dotted lines.*

A

After talking   a police   if it's believed   may be arrested

to them, a suspect   they disobey   been committed, or   a crime has

officer.

....

....

B

In some   handcuffs on them   people become   cases, often when

them to the police   violent, the police put   before taking   **station.**

....

....

C

At the placed offence is normally committed someone who's charged and a serious police station **in custody.**

D

There are the offender is serious, and or cause any considered less that are crimes, however, unlikely to reoffend in many of these **problems.**

E

In these due to stand they are be granted, and released until bail may situations, the person **trial.**

38. The Police

In the UK, the police have a lot of different jobs to do. They take turns to work day and night shifts so there are police officers on duty 24 hours a day. The police attend demonstrations and sports events to make sure they are peaceful, but when we see them in our cities and towns they're normally 'on patrol'. This means police officers in uniform drive or walk around the area they work in. When they're on foot, they speak to people in the community and find out what's happening. This gives them important information about the local area, and it reassures people that they are there to help and protect them. Anyone who sees them and is thinking of committing a crime is less likely to go ahead with it because they realise they may get caught.

*Complete the text by solving the puzzles (A-E) below. The first and last pieces of each puzzle, which are in **bold**, are in the right positions, but the others aren't! Put all the pieces into the correct order and write the words on the dotted lines.*

A

Another to calls about crimes public to respond police is for the responsibility from the **and accidents.**

....

....

B

They taking evidence and crime and witnesses, collecting victims of support, the speak to, and **statements.**

....

....

C

They people, property, of an investigation may technology or traditional out investigations be to search methods. Part also carry using the latest **vehicles or land.**

....

....

D

It's not administration as do a lot of they have to though, because detective work, all exciting **well.**

....

....

E

When they information put in a all the recorded and station has to be to the police get back **report.**

....

....

39. The Courts

A person who is charged with a criminal offence in the UK may be given bail, which means they can go home until they have to attend court and face a legal trial. For more serious offences, such as murder, rape and robbery, bail is not normally permitted. The person charged is kept in custody until the hearing, and when the trial takes place, it's held in a Crown Court. Someone being tried in court is referred to as the accused.

A trial is a formal examination of evidence by a judge and a jury. The judge is in charge and controls what happens in court, and the jury, twelve men and women who are members of the public, listen to everything said during the trial. They listen to the judge, experienced lawyers known as barristers, and any witnesses or other people who are asked to speak.

*Complete the text by solving the puzzles (A-E) below. The first and last pieces of each puzzle, which are in **bold**, are in the right positions, but the others aren't! Put all the pieces into the correct order and write the words on the dotted lines.*

A

One of accused by are therefore defends the a crime and haven't committed the barristers arguing they **innocent.**

....

....

B

The crime and are the accused by committed a prosecutes other barrister arguing they have **guilty.**

....

....

C

When the | is called | their decision, which | what they've | considered
jury have | reaching | heard, they make | **a verdict.**

D

If they | announces | accused is | they're guilty, the | conclude
what punishment is | and the judge | convicted | **to be given.**

E

If the jury | that they can | is acquitted, and | officially in court
innocent, the accused | the judge states | believe they're | **go free.**

40. Punishment and Prison

People who are charged with a crime have to go to court to be tried. If the accused is found guilty, the judge decides and then says what the punishment will be, which is called passing sentence. About three quarters of all sentences in the UK are fines, which are often for driving offences or theft. The amount of the fine depends on how much someone can pay and the seriousness of the crime, but it could be hundreds or thousands of pounds in some cases. If the accused is considered a danger to the public, or for more serious crimes, they are usually sent to prison for a period of time, and those guilty of murder can expect a 'life sentence', which means they'll be there for many years. In the UK, unlike some other countries, there is no death sentence. The death sentence for murder was abolished in 1965.

For less serious crimes, the punishment could be a suspended sentence. This is known as being put on probation. It means criminals won't go to prison if they behave well and don't reoffend. They also have to attend regular meetings with a probation officer for a period of time.

*Complete the text by solving the puzzles (A-E) below. The first and last pieces of each puzzle, which are in **bold**, are in the right positions, but the others aren't! Put all the pieces into the correct order and write the words on the dotted lines.*

A

Another   serious   community   for less   punishment   crimes is   **service.**

....

....

B

Community service   service   judge in court   community   done in the local   long the   local people. The   work which is   decides how   area to help   is unpaid   **should be.**

....

....

C

There are of them are UK than at any about 95% prison in the past, and more people in time in the **men.**

D

Many of very short either for are behind bars time or a these prisoners a long **time.**

E

About months or are in sentence, but are serving a prison for six almost 50% 20% of prisoners life **less.**

WORDS AND NUMBERS

41. English Grammar

Students who learn English spend much of their time studying English grammar. There are rules in English and all other languages which help us understand how to change the form of words and put words into the right order in sentences so they're grammatically correct. There are eight different types of word in the English language which all have a different function in a sentence and are called parts of speech. In alphabetical order, these are adjectives, adverbs, conjunctions, determiners, nouns, prepositions, pronouns and verbs. Teachers explain English grammar to students and give them examples and exercises once they've understood the rules.

*Complete the text by solving the puzzles (A-E) below. The first and last pieces of each puzzle, which are in **bold**, are in the right positions, but the others aren't! Put all the pieces into the correct order and write the words on the dotted lines.*

A

Before students   their lessons,   required to   and attend   the resources that are   English course   they think about   start their **do the course.**

....

....

B

They may   all these resources   books on grammar   to access   a dictionary and   unless they decide   choose to get   and vocabulary, **online.**

....

....

C

Students might not know where to to buy or information they what books find the **need online.**

D

If this is the case they their teacher, or who has helped ask for their could contact them register, and the person **advice.**

E

People working at the school course they're recommended or most what resources are suitable for the should be able to advise students **about to start.**

42. English Vocabulary

If English grammar is about changing words and putting them into the right place in a sentence, English vocabulary is about the meaning of words. It's about the meaning of all the words we use when we speak and write the English language. It takes time to learn a language, mainly because there are so many words to learn. A good question to ask is what we need to do to learn these words.

*Complete the text by solving the puzzles (A-E) below. The first and last pieces of each puzzle, which are in **bold**, are in the right positions, but the others aren't! Put all the pieces into the correct order and write the words on the dotted lines.*

A

Of   important   them   course, it's   pronounce   able to   to be **properly.**

....

....

B

However, we'll   vocabulary   understand what   them to our   learn and   to add   when we   only be able   **they mean.**

....

....

C

English   vocabulary exercises   giving students   them in English, and   words by explaining   students understand   teachers help   **to do.**

....

....

D

A lot of these in vocabulary books can use at online and they're home or take too, which students exercises are **to school.**

....

....

E

Whenever they or use a should make meaning of word up online sure they look the a word, they don't know the **dictionary.**

....

....

43. Words for Feelings

During our lives we experience a lot of different feelings and emotions. In the English language, words called adjectives are used to describe these emotions. People feel happy or sad, optimistic or pessimistic, proud or ashamed. When we have strong positive emotions, we are often very pleased or delighted, but if we experience strong negative emotions, we may feel angry or upset.

Some adjectives have two different endings. Adjectives which end -ed tell us how someone feels, but the same adjectives which end -ing say how someone or something is. So, for example, I was interested in watching a football match on TV because it should have been interesting, but nobody scored a goal. I got bored (this was how I felt), because the match was boring (how it was). I changed channels and started watching a film, but within minutes I was frightened. It was a frightening scene. Then I became terrified, because the film had become terrifying. I switched over again to the news, but started to feel depressed because the news was depressing. I was getting annoyed and irritated as well. The remote control wasn't working properly, which was annoying and irritating.

I decided to go to bed because I was tired after a tiring week at work. Then the phone rang. It was a friend who sounded very excited and had some exciting news.

*Complete the text by solving the puzzles (A-E) below. The first and last pieces of each puzzle, which are in **bold**, are in the right positions, but the others aren't! Put all the pieces into the correct order and write the words on the dotted lines.*

A

| **He'd been** | him why | seemed so | but he | he really wanted, |
| offered a job | surprised. I asked | | **it was surprising.** | |

....

....

B

| **He** | interview, which | him feel very | happened at the | embarrassing |
| that something | explained | made | **embarrassed.** | |

....

....

C

Someone over. The table, the floor he knocked it tea and all over the a cup of brought him tea went **and the wall.**

....

....

D

He was so convinced terribly disappointing which was the job, he wouldn't get himself disappointed. He'd **for him.**

....

....

E

When he story was so because the very amused laughing. I was couldn't stop happened, though, I told me what **amusing!**

....

....

44. Numbers and Calculations

When we want to talk about amounts or quantities, we use numbers. For instance, there are 75 centilitres of wine in a bottle, 31 days in March, and 52 playing cards in a pack. For large numbers which end with less than a hundred, the word 'and' is said before the number at the end. Using the number 23 as an example, we say one hundred and twenty-three and would also say one thousand and twenty-three, and one million and twenty-three! We do this with any combination of millions, thousands and hundreds. To give you an example of this, I've chosen two million, four thousand, one hundred and ten, which written as a number is 2,004,110. When we write numbers, they're written without any words, but there are commas after millions and thousands.

*Complete the text by solving the puzzles (A-E) below. The first and last pieces of each puzzle, which are in **bold**, are in the right positions, but the others aren't! Put all the pieces into the correct order and write the words on the dotted lines.*

A

For years such | two thousand | one up to | thousand and | tend to say two
of the century, we | the first decade | as those in | **and nine.**

B

After that, though, it's | numbers, so twenty | two numbers and
eleven, right up to | ten and twenty | common for us | then the second two
to say the first | **twenty ninety-nine.**

C

If we were to write the years 2009, 2010, 2011 and 2099. No commas are used for years as I've mentioned in numbers, we would write 2001, this paragraph as **written as numbers.**

D

Calculators on mobile phones make it easier to do calculations anywhere **and any time.**

E

In the English language we use the words 'plus, minus, times and divided by' for each of the main types of **calculation.**

45. Shapes and Sizes

If you want to describe an object, like a table or a window, you may need to mention its shape. Some of the most common shapes are rectangles, squares, triangles and circles. Half a circle is a semi-circle. These words are all nouns, but if you're thinking about a particular object, it's possible to use the adjectives, most of which are the same as the nouns except for the endings. You might, for instance, talk about a rectangular table, a square window, slices of pizza which are triangular, or describe wheels or roundabouts as circular or round.

There are many different ways of describing sizes, depending on what something is, as well as how small or how large it is. We use words for animals, objects and places, such as small, medium-sized or large. The smallest of these could be described as tiny, and the largest as enormous or huge.

*Complete the text by solving the puzzles (A-E) below. The first and last pieces of each puzzle, which are in **bold**, are in the right positions, but the others aren't! Put all the pieces into the correct order and write the words on the dotted lines.*

A

Clothes | used for eggs in | extra-large, | the largest | adjectives are | medium, large or | supermarkets, except | and the same | are small, | **are 'very large'.**

....

....

B

We also | measurements for | for dresses, socks | clothes, including | legs, and sizes | waist and | the collar, chest, | use numbers for | **and shoes.**

....

....

WORDS AND NUMBERS 91

C

In the UK, the capital letter A is used with a number for files, envelopes and pieces **of paper.**

D

Once you know it's A3 for the large ones, A4 for medium-sized ones, and A5 for smaller ones, you'll get the **right size.**

E

Whenever you look for something online, or in a shop, there are usually words, letters or numbers, or a combination of these, to help you find what **you want.**

SCIENCE

46. Biology

Biology is a science about things which are alive. In particular, it's about all the animals and plants on our planet. Many have similar features which enable us to put them into groups, such as class, order, family, genus and species. By doing this, animals and plants can be identified more easily and students can learn about them.

Biology students learn how animals and plants can only exist with the right habitats and ecosystems to support them. They're taught how life starts with reproduction, how genes are passed on to the next generation, and the role of DNA. They study the impact of hormones on growth, and how cells prevent disease by receiving and sending signals. They learn how nerves respond to touch, temperature, light and sound.

*Complete the text by solving the puzzles (A-E) below. The first and last pieces of each puzzle, which are in **bold**, are in the right positions, but the others aren't! Put all the pieces into the correct order and write the words on the dotted lines.*

A

Biology is also   other words, what   how it leaves   excretion, or in

inside, and then   digestion and   broken down   about nutrition,

body, how it's   goes into the   **the body.**

B

It's   and hydrogen, are   breathing, too, and   carbon dioxide

as oxygen,   about respiration and   how gases such   **essential to life.**

C

In animals, a circulation around needed everything transports blood **system.**

....

....

D

In plants, leaves, and food is the roots to the the leaves to the is moved from carried from water **rest of the plant.**

....

....

E

Whatever's a way of learning nature finds is a way of it, and biology required, providing **about it.**

....

....

47. Chemistry

Chemistry is the study of matter, which is really everything in the universe. Matter exists in different forms: solids, liquids, gases and plasma. It only changes when it's made to change by some outside force. If you add energy, such as heat, to a solid, it can become a liquid, and more energy can turn it into a gas. With a lot more heat, a gas changes to plasma. These changes from solids to plasma are all about groups of tiny things called atoms, which break away from each other and move further and further apart.

Everything around us is made up of atoms, so they're everywhere, but far too small for us to see them with our eyes. Inside every atom there are what could be described as dots of electricity called protons and neutrons, which are joined together. Amazingly, there are even smaller, lighter particles called electrons that move round them and are part of the atom. Substances whose atoms all have the same number of protons are called elements, and two or more elements joined together form a compound. When some elements and compounds come into contact, they form new substances, and either pure substances (one element or compound), or a mixture of pure substances, form matter.

*Complete the text by solving the puzzles (A-E) below. The first and last pieces of each puzzle, which are in **bold**, are in the right positions, but the others aren't! Put all the pieces into the correct order and write the words on the dotted lines.*

A

| **Chemists** | under different | substances. They want | substances react |
| reactions in | to know how | study chemical | **conditions.** |

....

....

B

| **They're** | with each | happens | in contact | combined or |
| interested | when they're | **other.** | | in what |

....

....

SCIENCE 95

C

There are almost everything study carbon and its who study chemists, who are inorganic chemists, compounds, and there organic **else.**

....

....

D

The polymer, on organic depend industries all and pharmaceutical petrochemical **chemists.**

....

....

E

There are discovered every compounds, and more chemists are busy millions of organic year, so these are invented or **people!**

....

....

48. Physics

Physics is the scientific study of energy and matter, and the interaction between them. It's the study of forces such as heat, light and sound, the relationships between them and how they affect objects. A force causes an object to change, and unbalanced forces cause changes in direction, shape or speed. The way everything moves, rises and falls, accelerates or slows down, can be explained by physics.

We rely on energy in everything we do. There's energy in moving objects, and potential energy in objects that aren't moving. There's energy in heat, light and sound, and in fuel, food and batteries. There are many forms of electrical energy as well. Electricity can be generated from fossil fuels and nuclear power, although it's non-renewable energy. It can also be generated from wind, water, geothermal and solar energy, and these are renewable forms of energy.

*Complete the text by solving the puzzles (A-E) below. The first and last pieces of each puzzle, which are in **bold**, are in the right positions, but the others aren't! Put all the pieces into the correct order and write the words on the dotted lines.*

A

We rely in stretched or energy every time even energy stored it off. There's on electromagnetic a light, or turn we switch on **squashed objects.**

....

....

B

Waves are different energy. They're vast amount also sources of generate a used in many ocean waves ways, and our **of energy.**

....

....

SCIENCE 97

C

They're and radiotherapy in   and radio signals,   for X-rays   phones, and ovens and mobile   used for TV   microwave   **hospitals.**

D

Of course,   waves, or radiation,   electromagnetic   it possible for is a mixture of   also make   us to see. Sunlight   light waves **from the sun.**

E

Physics   what happens on   explains much of   about the universe is extraordinary. It   many questions   Earth, and answers   **as well.**

49. Maths

The most common type of maths, which is the short form of the word 'mathematics', is arithmetic. Arithmetic is the operation of numbers in addition, subtraction, multiplication and division. Two or more numbers can be added, subtracted, multiplied or divided, and each calculation gives us a result. 'Plus, minus, times' and 'into' are other words which we use for these operations, and we put the word 'equals' before the number that we've calculated. All four operations and the word 'equals' are also represented by symbols, which are used much more than words in written calculations.

*Complete the text by solving the puzzles (A-E) below. The first and last pieces of each puzzle, which are in **bold**, are in the right positions, but the others aren't! Put all the pieces into the correct order and write the words on the dotted lines.*

A

Other types statistics, probability   as algebra, geometry,

and universities, such   taught in schools   of maths are   **and calculus.**

B

In algebra, letters   angles, surfaces   and relationships of lines,

do with the measurements   geometry is to   quantities, whereas

used to represent   and symbols are   **and solids.**

C

Statistics is all / which give us / a particular / shown in numbers
happening in / about information / of what is / a better idea / **situation.**

D

Probability, often / about the future / percentages, is / that something
and the chances / expressed in / **will happen.**

E

Calculus deals / population over / instance, in a / of a moving object
change, for / to the end of / time, or the speed / with rates of
from the start / a period of / **its movement.**

50. Computing

Whenever we use a computer, we give it a set of instructions, which is known as input. The computer then processes the input and produces a result, which is called output. On a PC, normal input is done by typing on a keyboard and clicking with a mouse, but using a camera and a scanner are other ways of doing it. On phones and tablets, input is carried out simply by touching the screen. The instructions then go to a microprocessor, which is the part of the computer that contains all the functions of the Central Processing Unit, or CPU. It's here that the information is processed. Once it's been processed, the output on a PC is usually shown on a screen, but output can also be sounds from speakers or a printed document from a printer. There are very different outputs from different computers.

Computers have both hardware and software. Computer hardware is all the physical parts of a computer that we can actually touch. We know about some of these parts, such as the computer case, monitor, keyboard and mouse. Other parts, though, are inside the case, so can only be seen if the computer is opened up.

*Complete the text by solving the puzzles (A-E) below. The first and last pieces of each puzzle, which are in **bold**, are in the right positions, but the others aren't! Put all the pieces into the correct order and write the words on the dotted lines.*

A

Inside a computer   the main memory   board, called   there's a plastic   the CPU and   which has   the motherboard,   **on it.**

....

....

B

There's   applications, and   and write   stores all the   disk drive which   also a hard   drive to read   an optical disk   and software   data files   **information.**

....

....

C

Unlike hardware, hardware and operate be touched. It's control the programs that all the computer software can't **the computer.**

D

Software is understand hardware can which the codes translated into **and process.**

E

Hardware computer. One essential to a are both work without couldn't and software **the other.**

HUMAN BEINGS

51. How We Think

One of the main differences between human beings and all other forms of life is our highly developed brain. In the early stages of development, we competed with other mammals and reptiles for food, and relied on our instincts to find enough to eat and stay alive. This started to change when we learnt to walk on two legs, and use our hands to do things. At the same time our brains grew larger and more intelligent. We became conscious of ourselves and our actions, and adapted to our environment.

Unlike animals, human beings have become creative, productive and resourceful. Our brains are capable of abstract thought, reasoning and planning.

*Complete the text by solving the puzzles (A-E) below. The first and last pieces of each puzzle, which are in **bold**, are in the right positions, but the others aren't! Put all the pieces into the correct order and write the words on the dotted lines.*

A

We have   about time,   think   memories, and   and right   death,   feelings and   life and   **and wrong.**

....

....

B

Our   enabled us   each   language has   and understand   use of   to communicate   **other.**

....

....

C

We appreciate beauty and humour, and self-control, personality, have **and pleasure.**

....

....

D

With powerful beings have advanced and developments, human the most these extraordinary creatures on become **the planet.**

....

....

E

With and the world life, the environment to protect a responsibility governments, have particular our of us, and in responsibility. All power, though, comes **we live in.**

....

....

52. How We Look

Identical twins look very similar, but most other people look different from each other. Our skin colour is so varied that no two individuals are the same. People are tall, short or medium height. There are thin or slim people, and others who are normal weight, or overweight. A healthy diet and regular exercise help us look fit and well. An unhealthy lifestyle, though, can make us look unfit and unwell.

Some people are thought to be good-looking or attractive. Good-looking women are frequently described as beautiful, girls as pretty, and men or boys as handsome. The negative tends to be used to say the opposite, so for example, that someone isn't good-looking.

People's hair is so different that we often mention it before anything else. Hair is naturally straight, curly or wavy. Some of us have short or medium length hair, and others grow their hair until it's long. The word for men who are losing their hair is 'balding', and men with little or no hair are bald. Hair can be a number of different colours, but most people in the world have black or brown hair. The rest have red, ginger or yellow hair, and someone with yellow hair is often described as blond.

*Complete the text by solving the puzzles (A-E) below. The first and last pieces of each puzzle, which are in **bold**, are in the right positions, but the others aren't! Put all the pieces into the correct order and write the words on the dotted lines.*

A

When many cases grey, and in older, their people get goes hair normally **turns white.**

....

....

B

There's side parting or as well, and of different hairstyles a wide variety centre parting, a the choice of a **a fringe.**

....

....

C

For hair, a plaits are with long people ponytail, bun or **options.**

D

Finally, although grow stubble, day, others a beard or a every men shave a lot of or have **moustache.**

E

With so look possibilities, no we all wonder many **different!**

106 GRAMMAR PUZZLES

53. How We Move

Human beings move around in different ways, so there are words in the English language for all the types of movement. Dancers dance, climbers climb and swimmers swim. Babies crawl and soldiers march. In most situations, children and adults walk from one place to another, but if we're in a hurry we sometimes run. Sports players jump to reach a ball, or a net, and athletes take part in the high jump, the long jump and the triple jump. When we visit a town or a city for the first time, many of us like to take a stroll and wander round. Whenever we go for a walk, though, it's important to take care and watch where we're going. If we don't, we could trip over something, and when there's ice or there are wet leaves on the ground, it's easy to slip and fall. Anyone who falls and hurts a foot or a leg might not be able to walk normally. When this happens, they may walk with a limp.

We move other parts of our bodies even when we're not walking.

*Complete the text by solving the puzzles (A-E) below. The first and last pieces of each puzzle, which are in **bold**, are in the right positions, but the others aren't! Put all the pieces into the correct order and write the words on the dotted lines.*

A

We stretch   exercise, and we   we get   arms, or cross   morning, or before   and legs when   often fold our   up in the   our arms **our legs.**

....

....

B

We turn our   hand and point   shrug our   wave with a   heads and shoulders. We   **with a finger.**

....

....

C

We lean down, carry it wall, bend our up, put it or against a somewhere, throw forwards, backwards knees, pick something **it or catch it.**

D

Sometimes move them even want we don't when our bodies **to.**

E

We tremble gives us or something jump when someone with cold, and with fear, shiver **a shock!**

54. How We Sound

We use our voices to make sounds and communicate with other people. In most situations we talk or speak to someone. There are other sounds we make, though, whenever we experience and are affected by strong emotions or feelings. We laugh when something is funny or hilarious, and young children often giggle. We cry when we're very unhappy, happy or sad, or feel deep sympathy. We groan if we're annoyed, upset or in pain, and sigh with relief, sadness or frustration. We yawn when we're bored or tired, and puff and pant if we're exhausted and out of breath.

*Complete the text by solving the puzzles (A-E) below. The first and last pieces of each puzzle, which are in **bold**, are in the right positions, but the others aren't! Put all the pieces into the correct order and write the words on the dotted lines.*

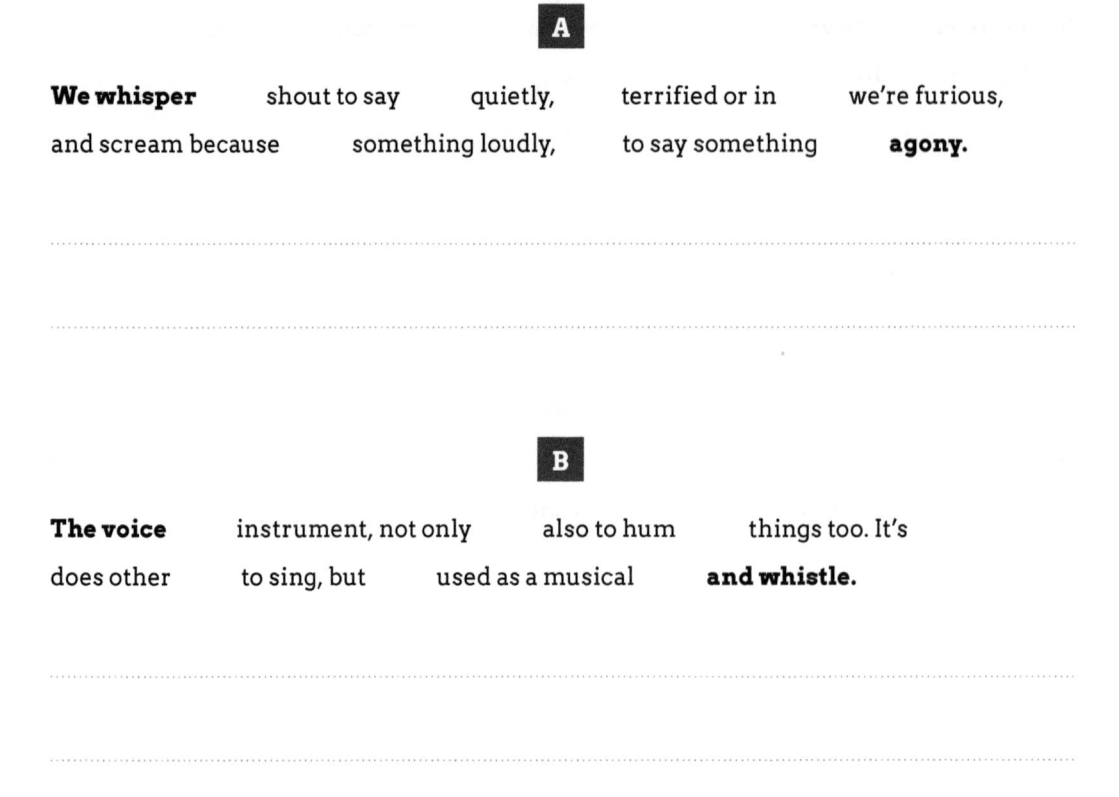

A

We whisper   shout to say   quietly,   terrified or in   we're furious,
and scream because   something loudly,   to say something   **agony.**

....

....

B

The voice   instrument, not only   also to hum   things too. It's
does other   to sing, but   used as a musical   **and whistle.**

....

....

C

We intend we don't normally are other sounds sounds, but there make on to make these **purpose.**

....

....

D

Anyone with we sometimes drink some cough, babies again until we sneeze or a cold might hiccup again and burp, and **water.**

....

....

E

There's one asleep some of us unaware of. When we're we're almost always sound, though, that we wake other snore so loudly **people up!**

....

....

55. Communication

We normally communicate by talking to people, but there are numerous forms of non-verbal communication too. For many of these we use our faces, or our faces give information to others. Most of the time we intend this to happen, but it's a form of communication that may not be intended, and we may not even be aware it's happening! The expressions on our faces tell other people how we're feeling. When we're happy or amused, we smile with our mouths and with our eyes. We open our mouths and yawn when we're bored or tired, and may also open them if we're surprised or amazed. We blush when we're ashamed or embarrassed, and put our hands over our mouths when we're shocked or horrified.

We use our eyes in many different ways as well. If we feel very emotional, many of us cry, and tears come out of our eyes. We glance at something to check it and stare at someone or something if we're thinking about them. Have you ever used your eyes to wink at someone when you wanted to share a joke or a secret? Can you remember the last time you were dazzled by bright light, and it made you blink? How do you react when you're surprised? Do you raise your eyebrows?

We frequently use gestures with our heads or our hands to give information to others. These gestures are also forms of non-verbal communication. We shake our heads to disagree with someone or say 'no', and nod to agree or say 'yes'.

*Complete the text by solving the puzzles (A-E) below. The first and last pieces of each puzzle, which are in **bold**, are in the right positions, but the others aren't! Put all the pieces into the correct order and write the words on the dotted lines.*

A

| **We raise a** | to be | of our | want someone | in front | when we |
| mouths | finger | **quiet.** | | | |

....

....

B

We clap a finger, and knock at something with know we're at
our hands, point and wave with to let someone **the door.**

C

In the means that upwards, it good or it's thumb
something's point a UK, if we **gone well.**

D

If we it's gone it's bad, or it means it downwards, point
badly.

E

A gesture when you use be careful another country, so could have
meaning in a different **them abroad!**

LIFE

56. Having a Baby

When a woman is pregnant it means she's going to have a baby. It's normally about nine months before she gives birth. Being pregnant can be a difficult time for a woman, and there's a lot to learn. Doctors and nurses at the local health centre are able to give advice. There are also ante-natal classes, and there's information online for women and their partners, which makes it easier for them. They learn about having a baby, and looking after it when it's very young and small. Most women suffer from morning sickness, which makes them feel sick, and in some cases vomit, in the early months of pregnancy. Although it's called morning sickness, women may be unwell at any time of day, but they normally feel better by the fourteenth week.

The period of time just before a woman gives birth is called labour. For a first baby, labour usually takes about eight hours, but it could be much shorter or longer. (11)

*Complete the text by solving the puzzles (A-E) below. The first and last pieces of each puzzle, which are in **bold**, are in the right positions, but the others aren't! Put all the pieces into the correct order and write the words on the dotted lines.*

A

When a woman   have her baby at   hospital as soon   she's decided to   needs to be   taken to   goes into labour, she   as possible, unless   **home.**

....

....

B

Most women   after the   ward of a hospital   during, and   maternity   of time, before,   stay in the   for the period   choose to   **baby is born.**

....

....

C

It's reassuring to know for them specialists, such as doctors and midwives, in there are medical **the building.**

D

These all the medical equipment needed, and places also have women who are drugs are available to help **in pain.**

E

If anything goes resources to deal safest has more problem, so wrong, a hospital it's usually the with the **place to be.**

57. Children

It's amazing how quickly children develop when they're very young. In the first six months of life, babies cry, laugh and make other sounds. They move their eyes, and raise their legs and their heads. After a year, they sit and crawl, and may be able to stand, and after two years, they know how to walk, and then to run. When they're about four, they learn to walk up and down stairs, and a year later they can dance.

At the same time, children's minds are also developing. When they're two years old, they're capable of saying a few words, and before long they know about fifty words and their own name. At three, they ask questions that begin with 'what, where' and 'who', and can draw a person with a head. Adults understand children who are four years old, and their vocabulary is normally about 1500 words by this age.

*Complete the text by solving the puzzles (A-E) below. The first and last pieces of each puzzle, which are in **bold**, are in the right positions, but the others aren't! Put all the pieces into the correct order and write the words on the dotted lines.*

A

Their heads, legs   of people with   able to draw   soon they're   drawings are now   and arms, and   **a house.**

....

....

B

When they're age and their   their fingers, and   including their   about themselves,   to count using   five, they learn   they know more   **birthday.**

....

....

C

They've already   a few letters of   how to write   about this age
copy squares   speak, and it's   learnt how to   the alphabet, and
that they learn   **and triangles.**

D

Children go   they become   stages of   time they're   through several
development, from the   born to the time   **teenagers.**

E

At each   place in the early   quickly, but the   school, are   they go to
stage they develop   years, before   changes that take   **amazing!**

116 GRAMMAR PUZZLES

58. Growing Up

Being a teenager isn't easy. Young people have to deal with all sorts of experiences. Their bodies grow quickly and change shape. They experience strong feelings and thoughts, which make them behave differently from before. They begin to understand more about who they are, being an individual and having an identity. They want to be liked by other children at school, and worry that they may not be. As they grow older, they learn more about love and sex as well, and who they are attracted to. Many argue with their parents. This stage of development is difficult for most young people and can be unhappy and painful. The good news is that it only lasts a few years.

As they get older, teenagers rely less on their parents and start to become more independent. Teenagers in the UK have to go to school, so they spend most of their time with people their own age. They learn the same things and share similar views of the world.

*Complete the text by solving the puzzles (A-E) below. The first and last pieces of each puzzle, which are in **bold**, are in the right positions, but the others aren't! Put all the pieces into the correct order and write the words on the dotted lines.*

A

They and words   the world they   vocabulary   their own   choose to describe   **are in.**

....

....

B

There are so   parents used to   them, but not   to make. Their   these decisions for   many new decisions   make most of   **any longer.**

....

....

C

They free time, or sports to do in their drink, what and what games eat and decide what to **to play.**

....

....

D

They what music phone or wear, on the to chat with clothes to and who choose what to listen to, **Internet.**

....

....

E

They do makes them they decide to friends. What to make when and how they like, and decide who **who they are.**

....

....

59. Adults

Adults have a lot of decisions to make. They decide what to do when they leave school. Some choose to work, others go to college or university. What job should they do, and where should they do it? Do they drive, cycle, walk, or take public transport? They make decisions about relationships, who they spend time with, and who their friends are. Do they stay single, live with someone, or get married? They decide whether to have children, or adopt children, and how many to have. Over the years and the decades, couples choose to stay together, split up or get divorced.

Would they prefer to be in a city, a town, or the countryside? Adults decide where to live, and whether they should rent or buy a flat or a house, with or without a garden. Do they have pets, and if so, what kind, and how many? They choose their furniture, and how their home should look. What food do they eat and what do they drink? Do they recycle, or throw things away? They decide where to go shopping, what to buy, what clothes and shoes to wear, what hairstyle to have. Where should they travel to, or go on holiday, and what do they do when they get there?

*Complete the text by solving the puzzles (A-E) below. The first and last pieces of each puzzle, which are in **bold**, are in the right positions, but the others aren't! Put all the pieces into the correct order and write the words on the dotted lines.*

A

Adults　where to　money and　their　to spend　how　choose **save it.**

....

....

B

They follow　decisions about　play and their　team. They make party, or a sports　a religion, a political　the sports they　**pastimes.**

....

....

C

What type to? Do they decide radio programme if so, what do time reading, and of music or to spend should they listen **they read?**

D

What TV media they're plays should when to call, email choose the social in, and who and channels, films, or interested they watch? They **or text.**

....

....

E

It can't very grown-up so many world. They must be in the modern to make being an adult be easy **decisions!**

....

....

60. Education

In England, some children go to nursery school when they're very young, and most children go to primary school by the time they're six years old. When they're eleven or twelve, they leave primary school and go to secondary school, where they usually study a number of subjects. They take exams in these subjects in their mid-teens, usually at the age of sixteen, and the qualifications they get if they pass are called GCSEs, which is short for General Certificate in Secondary Education. The subjects they do usually include English, maths, and science (biology, chemistry and physics), as well as history, geography, and design and technology.

After GCSEs it's possible for people to leave school and try to find work. Those who want to continue their education can apply to go to a college to study a particular subject. The subject they choose may be related to a type of work, so it could eventually help them get a job. The other option is to stay at the same school, or move to a different school, and do a two-year course called A levels (short for Advanced levels).

Students who decide to do A levels normally study between two and four subjects.

*Complete the text by solving the puzzles (A-E) below. The first and last pieces of each puzzle, which are in **bold**, are in the right positions, but the others aren't! Put all the pieces into the correct order and write the words on the dotted lines.*

A

The   are often   they took   choose   well in when   they did subjects they   the ones   **their GCSEs.**

....

....

B

If they get   be offered   the country's   grades in their   course at one of good enough   a place on a   A levels, they may   **universities.**

....

....

C

After three a degree in their graduate from of study, assessment
means they gain or four years university, which and exams, students
subject.

....

....

D

All the hard school, at college, gained, are the qualifications they've
done at work they've or at university, and **important.**

....

....

E

It could all be only when careers as in their future them, not
a great help to they start work, but **well.**

....

....

WORK

61. Finding Work

Young adults are faced with challenges and responsibilities that can be very stressful and difficult. When they leave school or university, they need to decide what to do with their lives. Most people choose to look for a job and spend a period of time trying to find the right one. To be successful they need to convince an employer they have more to offer than the other candidates. Good qualifications achieved in education are important, but an employer often requires experience as well.

In an increasingly competitive market, it's very difficult to find the dream job.

*Complete the text by solving the puzzles (A-E) below. The first and last pieces of each puzzle, which are in **bold**, are in the right positions, but the others aren't! Put all the pieces into the correct order and write the words on the dotted lines.*

A

It's often   temporary   well   to apply for a   that isn't as   more realistic   or a job   better and   position   **paid.**

....

....

B

By doing this   the opportunity   the experience   chance of   and gaining   there's a better   getting   to work   **needed.**

....

....

C

People hard, get things jobs can show an important part they work their employer in temporary done, and are **of a team.**

....

....

D

Some of promotion and position and get a or more senior same company a better paid with the them stay others find **elsewhere.**

....

....

E

Whatever the have been initial will usually of employment outcome is, the period **very helpful.**

....

....

124 GRAMMAR PUZZLES

62. Employment

If you want to find a job, you may need to complete an application form or a CV. A CV gives information about your personal details, education, training and previous employment. When you send this information to an employer, which can be done either directly or via an employment website, the employer will assess your qualifications and experience, and decide whether you should be shortlisted for the position.

*Complete the text by solving the puzzles (A-E) below. The first and last pieces of each puzzle, which are in **bold**, are in the right positions, but the others aren't! Put all the pieces into the correct order and write the words on the dotted lines.*

A

If you are　　questions　　candidates, or　　interview where　　as other　　attend an　　the same　　invited to　　you'll be asked　　shortlisted, you'll be **similar questions.**

....

....

B

The interview　　which is vacant,　　for recruitment,　　of the position　　officer responsible　　line manager　　resources　　conducted by the　　or by a human　　may be　　**or both.**

....

....

C

If you do should you decide benefits you'll receive job, and you'll be offered the interview you may well at the be told what **to accept.**

....

....

D

Some also get annual employees, and a salary, you'll to new receiving courses offer training apart from companies **leave.**

....

....

E

You years later means plan too, which pension many pension given a able to join a when you will be you'll be **retire.**

....

....

126 GRAMMAR PUZZLES

63. Interviews

Getting the job you want can be difficult. A lot of unemployed people are looking for work. To be successful you have to do better than other people who apply for the position. An employer wants to know you have the right skills, experience and motivation to do a professional job. You need to convince them you have what's required. Think about what you should write in your application.

What can you do to have the best chance? First of all, read about the company online so you learn more about it, and what it does. Make sure you know and understand all the words and expressions that you need to talk about the job. If you're invited to go for an interview, there should be an opportunity to impress the interviewer with your knowledge of the work you would do, and the company you've applied to join. It's also very important to let the interviewer know about any experience you've had that could help you do the job. Think carefully about the personal qualities you've got that could be useful, and what motivates you to do well.

*Complete the text by solving the puzzles (A-E) below. The first and last pieces of each puzzle, which are in **bold**, are in the right positions, but the others aren't! Put all the pieces into the correct order and write the words on the dotted lines.*

A

What else | to offer | encourage them | you ask at | questions will | them that will | position? What | can you tell | you the | **the end?**

....

....

B

Your appearance | company and | time deciding | the job, the | too. Spend | it's right for | is important | wear, so | what to | **the occasion.**

....

....

C

Start your journey early so you're not in a hurry, and you arrive ready when you are calm and **at reception.**

D

Employers don't like people to be late for your appointment! work, so they won't be happy if you're late for **appointment!**

E

Finally, during the interview, listen carefully, be positive and enthusiastic and answer the questions in a relaxed, be confident, **way.**

64. People at Work

Some people are self-employed, but the majority of workers are employed by companies or organisations. Jobs in these companies can be either temporary or permanent, but nowadays it's very unusual for a job to be for life. Positions are full-time, which would normally be at least 35 hours a week, or part-time, if the work can be done in fewer hours or days of the week. Most people have their own jobs, but they also work as part of a team with other people, who are their colleagues.

*Complete the text by solving the puzzles (A-E) below. The first and last pieces of each puzzle, which are in **bold**, are in the right positions, but the others aren't! Put all the pieces into the correct order and write the words on the dotted lines.*

A

Employees	manager, who	companies is	managing	a more senior
who in larger	to a manager,	might be a	accountable to	report
director.				

....

....

B

Companies	sales, another	position, often a	job is in	financial
person whose	someone in a	least one	in marketing, and	
usually have at	**qualified accountant.**			

....

....

C

Other employees deal with human resources, or information technology, or relations, or HR, public PR, and **or IT.**

D

There's normally a customer services person or team as well, to help resolve any **problems.**

E

By employing people with most different skills, knowledge and experience, companies are usually well placed to deal with everyday issues and work **tasks.**

65. Jobs

I recently asked the students in one of my classes what jobs they wanted to do when they left London and returned to their countries to find work.

*Complete the text by solving the puzzles (A-E) below. The first and last pieces of each puzzle, which are in **bold**, are in the right positions, but the others aren't! Put all the pieces into the correct order and write the words on the dotted lines.*

A

Many of our | jobs while they're | waiters and | working as | are temporary
students are | baristas, but these | au pairs, cleaners, | **in the UK.**

....

....

B

What they | doing now, are | of them are | the jobs some | career, and
to do as a | would really like | **very different.**

....

....

C

I asked | occupations that | question | interested | other about the
think about the | talking to each | minutes, before | my students to
for a few | **them.**

....

....

D

These are some of the careers they were interested in: interior designer, engineer, IT specialist, accountant, farmer, estate agent, chef, architect, receptionist, journalist, and **dentist.**

E

They're all jobs that people can hope to get and be successful in, provided they have the right qualifications, skills, **and experience.**

132 LEISURE

66. The Arts

Art, literature, music and theatre are often called the Arts, especially when we talk about them as a group. Art is a subject which can be studied at school, college or university. We go to art galleries or museums to see the visual arts: paintings, drawings, and ceramics by famous artists, and photographs taken by well-known photographers. Some forms of visual art are located outdoors and have become tourist attractions. Beautiful buildings designed by architects, statues, and other sculptures, can be viewed in the parks and squares of our cities and towns.

Literature refers to any written work which is considered to be artistic or intellectual because it's different from the ordinary language in everyday use. It comprises works of fiction; the novels, plays, poems and short stories created in the imagination of the writer. It also includes works of non-fiction; books about real people, events, and established fact, like biographies.

*Complete the text by solving the puzzles (A-E) below. The first and last pieces of each puzzle, which are in **bold**, are in the right positions, but the others aren't! Put all the pieces into the correct order and write the words on the dotted lines.*

A

The theatre | known as a | plays are | theatre is often | is why | performed, which | is where | **performing art.**

....

....

B

Cinema, | arts, because | also called | in front of | or performers perform | music concerts are | these, the artists | in all of | dance and | performing | opera, ballet, | **an audience.**

....

....

C

Music is and films as music is a very almost all the it's used in plays some concerts, and of opera, ballet and featured in important part performances. Classical **well.**

D

There are performances, but music, though, by people at played in public types of many other are also enjoyed which are **home.**

E

When an art form sing, dance, or play available to music, when we form or another, is instrument, we experience we listen to which, in one a musical **everyone.**

67. Entertainment

Entertainment is about providing or showing something interesting or amusing to people. It's for people to enjoy, and in the modern world it's also about making money. Many of us in the UK still go to the cinema, to sports events, music concerts, nightclubs and comedy clubs, but most forms of entertainment are now experienced at home.

Some of the most popular forms of entertainment are watching films or TV programmes, listening to music and reading books. Technology has changed the way we experience and enjoy entertainment. Information on the Internet and computer games are two examples of this, but almost any form of entertainment is now available online. Just as there are numerous types of music, there are also many different types of film, known as genres. These include action films, horror films, romantic films, comedies and thrillers.

Complete the text by solving the puzzles (A-E) below. The first and last pieces of each puzzle, which are in **bold**, are in the right positions, but the others aren't! Put all the pieces into the correct order and write the words on the dotted lines.

A

Most of   written and published   were originally   on stories that   of fiction and   or other works   as novels, biographies,   are based   these films   **non-fiction.**

....

....

B

Films, current   TV every   comedy series   affairs programmes,   are shown on   events, drama and   sports   **day.**

....

....

C

There's also a large variety of other programmes, including soap operas, quiz shows, and **documentaries.**

D

In the 1960s there were only three TV channels: BBC1, BBC2 **and ITV.**

E

Nowadays there are so many channels, in fact, that when we switch on the TV, we often can't decide what **to watch!**

68. Music

There are many different types of music, some of which originated much longer ago than others. People have enjoyed listening to classical music and jazz for centuries, and country music has existed since the 1920s. Pop, reggae, soul, and R&B, have all been popular for at least fifty years, as have rock and disco. In recent decades, hip hop, rap, dance, and techno, amongst others, have also become popular.

Most musicians who perform these types of music are either solo artists, or in groups and bands. Some of them are vocalists, and others play a large variety of instruments, such as the guitar, the drums and keyboards. Classical musicians, who play instruments like the violin and the piano, may decide to join an orchestra. Jazz musicians, whose instruments include the saxophone, the trumpet and the double bass, often play as members of a jazz band.

Some people learn to play a musical instrument, and others have singing lessons. Those lucky enough to have good voices can sing on their own, or with other people (in a group of singers, or a choir).

*Complete the text by solving the puzzles (A-E) below. The first and last pieces of each puzzle, which are in **bold**, are in the right positions, but the others aren't! Put all the pieces into the correct order and write the words on the dotted lines.*

A

A few of the front of audiences, musicians, who or sing in musical instruments talented eventually become play their best and most **famous and wealthy.**

....

....

B

Successful studio to record to have a played on the these were and go to a musicians tended their songs, and recording contract **radio and on TV.**

....

....

C

Times have or laptop music can be to on a desktop though. Nowadays of it is listened downloaded and much changed, **computer.**

....

....

D

Most instruments as only people musical play **a pastime.**

....

....

E

They and friends, usually their own, or fun and they play music on because it's for their family **enjoy it.**

....

....

69. Hobbies

A hobby is an activity that people do to relax or for pleasure in their free time. When adults aren't working, and children aren't at school, a lot of us spend time on our hobbies. Most hobbies used to take place at home, but computers and technology have made it possible for many of these activities to be done anywhere, indoors or outdoors. We watch TV and films and listen to music on public transport. We use social media and play games in coffee shops and parks. Traditional games like Monopoly, Scrabble and chess were once played on boards, and crosswords and puzzles were in newspapers and books. Nowadays they can all be played or done on screens. People used to do creative writing with pens and paper, but most of it now is done using a keyboard.

There are creative hobbies, though, that haven't changed that much, such as painting, drawing, cooking and playing musical instruments.

*Complete the text by solving the puzzles (A-E) below. The first and last pieces of each puzzle, which are in **bold**, are in the right positions, but the others aren't! Put all the pieces into the correct order and write the words on the dotted lines.*

A

Some   collecting coins   clothes, jewellery   things, too, like

of us enjoy making   and models, and   **and stamps.**

....

....

B

A number   necessary part of   outdoors is an   place outdoors

of pastimes   because being   important or   usually take   **the activity.**

....

....

C

Gardening and flying kites, are all outdoor activities, as well as camping, fishing and metal detecting, for example.

....

....

D

Walking, sailing, and golf are all hobbies too, and are normally outdoor sports, but they're activities for the **same reasons**.

....

....

E

Most other sports, though, can be played either inside at a leisure or sports **centre**, outside, or

....

....

140 GRAMMAR PUZZLES

70. Sports and Places

Tennis and badminton are played on a court with a net in the middle. In tennis you hit a ball over the net, but in badminton you hit a shuttlecock over the net (which is higher than a tennis net). Squash is also played on a court which looks like a large, empty room, and you hit a ball against the front wall. So is basketball, but the aim is to throw or drop a ball into a basket at the end that you're attacking and the other team is defending. It's not easy to do this, though, because the top of the basket is ten feet, or just over three metres, above the ground. Football, rugby and cricket are all played on large areas of short grass which are called pitches. In football and rugby, the pitches are rectangular, but in cricket they're circular. In football there are goals with nets at both ends, and in rugby there are posts at both ends in the shape of the letter 'H'.

*Complete the text by solving the puzzles (A-E) below. The first and last pieces of each puzzle, which are in **bold**, are in the right positions, but the others aren't! Put all the pieces into the correct order and write the words on the dotted lines.*

A

If you go   normally be   professionals, the   a pitch inside   played by
these sports   a stadium with   venue would   to watch   **the stadium.**

....

....

B

There   racing takes   sports. Horse   for other   venues, though,
are different   a golf   played on   and golf is   racecourse   place at a
course.

....

....

C

We can a building called track, and racing at a race at an athletics cycling track or in track, motor cycling at a watch athletics **a velodrome.**

D

We swim and play sports and leisure at one end, and pools, some in swimming water polo there are pools in with diving boards **centres.**

E

Whatever we can somewhere usually to do, there's we want **do it!**

THINGS

71. Sports Equipment

If you want to play a sport, you need to have the right equipment. For tennis, table tennis or squash, you need a racket and some balls, and if you play badminton, you need a racket and a shuttlecock. For a sport like football or rugby, you'll have to find a pair of boots that are the right size and a ball that's the right shape; a football is round and a rugby ball is more of an oval shape. You wear a swimsuit, or swimming trunks for swimming, and for cycling you'll need to buy a helmet and a bicycle, which is expensive. The equipment you need for golf can also be expensive because you have to buy about ten clubs, a bag to put them in, and plenty of golf balls.

A sport which is very popular in the UK, but you may never have played in your own country, is cricket. To play cricket you need a cricket ball, a cricket bat to hit the ball with (or bat with), a helmet and a pair of pads.

*Complete the text by solving the puzzles (A-E) below. The first and last pieces of each puzzle, which are in **bold**, are in the right positions, but the others aren't! Put all the pieces into the correct order and write the words on the dotted lines.*

A

The helmet is   protect your   pads   and the   your head
used to protect   are used to   **legs.**

....

....

B

There   team,   players in a   is called   of the players   are eleven
and one   **a wicket keeper.**

....

....

C

The wicket made of equipment behind a piece which is keeper stands wicket, called a **of wood.**

D

He, or two pairs only player who needs she, is the in the team **of gloves.**

E

One keep and a much to bat with, is to pair is larger pair **wicket with!**

144　GRAMMAR PUZZLES

72. Tools

A tool is an object that you hold in your hand and use to repair, make things, or do something else with. Hammers and screwdrivers are two of the most useful tools. In many homes they're kept in a container called a toolbox. Hammers are normally used to put nails into pieces of wood. A screwdriver is usually used to put a screw into a piece of wood, metal or plastic. Most of us have a hammer and at least one screwdriver at home.

Metal detectors aren't used to fix or make anything, but they are tools, and they have a number of different uses, some of them extraordinary. They're used during and after wars to find landmines, and at airports and other places to check people's bags. They're also used in buildings to locate metal pipes and other objects hidden above ceilings, below floors or behind walls. Metal detecting has become a popular pastime too.

*Complete the text by solving the puzzles (A-E) below. The first and last pieces of each puzzle, which are in **bold**, are in the right positions, but the others aren't! Put all the pieces into the correct order and write the words on the dotted lines.*

A

People　wherever　beaches, gardens　of metal　including fields, made　they might be,　for objects　enjoy looking　they think **and parks.**

....

....

B

Most metal　nails, aren't　tops and　of any real　objects in bottle　the ground, like　**interest.**

....

....

C

When exciting for the valuable is it can be very person who unusual or discovered, though, something old, **finds it.**

....

....

D

Metal objects and detect of gold, silver can made detectors **bronze.**

....

....

E

They've hundreds of as rings, of which are jewellery such coins, some used to find often been earrings and **years old!**

....

....

146 GRAMMAR PUZZLES

73. Work and School

I work in an office. I keep a lot of useful things in my office that I use every day and which help me do my job. I've got a desk with drawers that contain a wide variety of stationery. Nowadays diaries and calendars are available online, but I like to have manual ones in my office as well. I keep my diary in the top drawer of my desk, together with highlighters, paperclips, scissors, a ruler, a stapler and a notebook. There's plenty of room in the bottom drawer of my desk for some of the larger items, such as packets of A4 paper, and envelopes of different sizes. I've got a briefcase too, which I bring to work with me in the morning and take home in the evening. Everything else I need to do my job I tend to have in my briefcase, including a pencil case. I keep a sharpener, an eraser and a correction pen in the case, as well pens and pencils, so wherever I am I've always got something to write with. My children have many of these things at school and use some of them during their classes. Their stationery's much more colourful than mine!

*Complete the text by solving the puzzles (A-E) below. The first and last pieces of each puzzle, which are in **bold**, are in the right positions, but the others aren't! Put all the pieces into the correct order and write the words on the dotted lines.*

A

My laptop, desk. On one side has all my all on my a cupboard that calendar are phone and a printer, of the desk there's **files in it.**

B

On the other cardboard, and else that can put rubbish in, for paper, small bin to side, I keep a anything and larger ones **be recycled.**

C

Outside my meeting leads to other there's a office
corridor which offices and a **room.**

D

The meeting chart in one table in it, a has a large, round
the corridor, corner, and a coffee the end of the wall, a flip
room, which is at whiteboard on **machine in another.**

E

When try to make of coffee, before we usually start doing, and
meetings, we we have work we're talk about the with a cup
decisions!

74. Bathroom Things

There are lots of things in the bathroom that help me get ready every morning. Most them are above, below, or next to the basin. The hot and cold taps are just above the basin, which we fill with water whenever we want to wash our faces or hands.

I keep a tube of toothpaste, my toothbrush, a flannel and some soap beside the basin. There's also a razor and some shaving foam that I use to shave, and a mirror above the basin so I can see what I'm doing! It's on the front of the bathroom cabinet, which is on the wall, and has a lot of useful things in it. Inside the bathroom cabinet, on the top shelf, I keep a small pair of scissors, a few plasters in case I cut myself, and a tube of antiseptic cream to stop the cut becoming infected.

*Complete the text by solving the puzzles (A-E) below. The first and last pieces of each puzzle, which are in **bold**, are in the right positions, but the others aren't! Put all the pieces into the correct order and write the words on the dotted lines.*

A

On the bottle of scent, me, and a of aftershave, for that my wife called perfume, there's a bottle bottom shelf which is sometimes **uses.**

....

....

B

I keep my arms, a hairbrush well, including a comb if I want I use under my hair, and a so I can brush deodorant, which shelf as on the bottom other things **to comb it.**

....

....

C

Below the where we shower of shampoo, and a cupboard rolls, bottles basin there's keep toilet **gel.**

D

We keep out of well, in soap and toothpaste there as packets of case we run **anything.**

E

This is we go I put everything I put my in whenever also where washbag which **away.**

75. Kitchen Things

When we get back from the supermarket, we carry everything into the kitchen, and start taking food out of our shopping bags. Any frozen food goes into the freezer, and we put all our fresh food, such as vegetables, fruit and dairy products, in the fridge. Tinned food, cans of drinks and anything else that won't go off are stored in the larder, which is normally cool, but not cold like the fridge.

The meals we have every day are prepared in the kitchen. We use the large oven in the cooker to roast or bake food, the microwave oven to heat it or for ready meals, and the hob when food needs to be boiled or fried. Once we've finished eating, we sometimes do the washing up in the sink with a dishcloth and dry everything with a tea towel. Most of the time, though, we use the dishwasher.

*Complete the text by solving the puzzles (A-E) below. The first and last pieces of each puzzle, which are in **bold**, are in the right positions, but the others aren't! Put all the pieces into the correct order and write the words on the dotted lines.*

A

When we | shelves between | or on long | dishwasher, it's | out of the
in two cupboards, | take crockery | all put away | **the cupboards.**

....

....

B

We keep | glasses for | of the cupboards, and | drinks in the
and cups in one | and soft | water, wine | our mugs | **other.**

....

....

C

Plates, arranged saucers are of the on one bowls and **shelves.**

D

Below the utensils and prepare most our kitchen containing all the surface we a worktop, which is and drawers shelves there's of our food on, **cutlery.**

E

Under the drawers it. Whatever tray in a place for it cupboard which has there's a large pan and a baking it is, there's our saucepans, a frying **in our kitchen!**

HOMES

76. Finding Accommodation

When someone arrives in a city or town for the first time, they need to find accommodation, which is somewhere to stay or to live. They may be able to stay with friends or find a room in a house and become a lodger. If they don't know anyone, they should contact an estate agent, who can help them find a property to rent, usually a flat or a house. If it's a flat, it's important to know whether it's a basement flat, a ground floor flat, or a first, second or third floor flat. Of course, if it's in a large block of flats it could be much higher up. There would probably be a lift in the building and there may be a panoramic view (a view of a wide area of land), from one or more of the windows.

*Complete the text by solving the puzzles (A-E) below. The first and last pieces of each puzzle, which are in **bold**, are in the right positions, but the others aren't! Put all the pieces into the correct order and write the words on the dotted lines.*

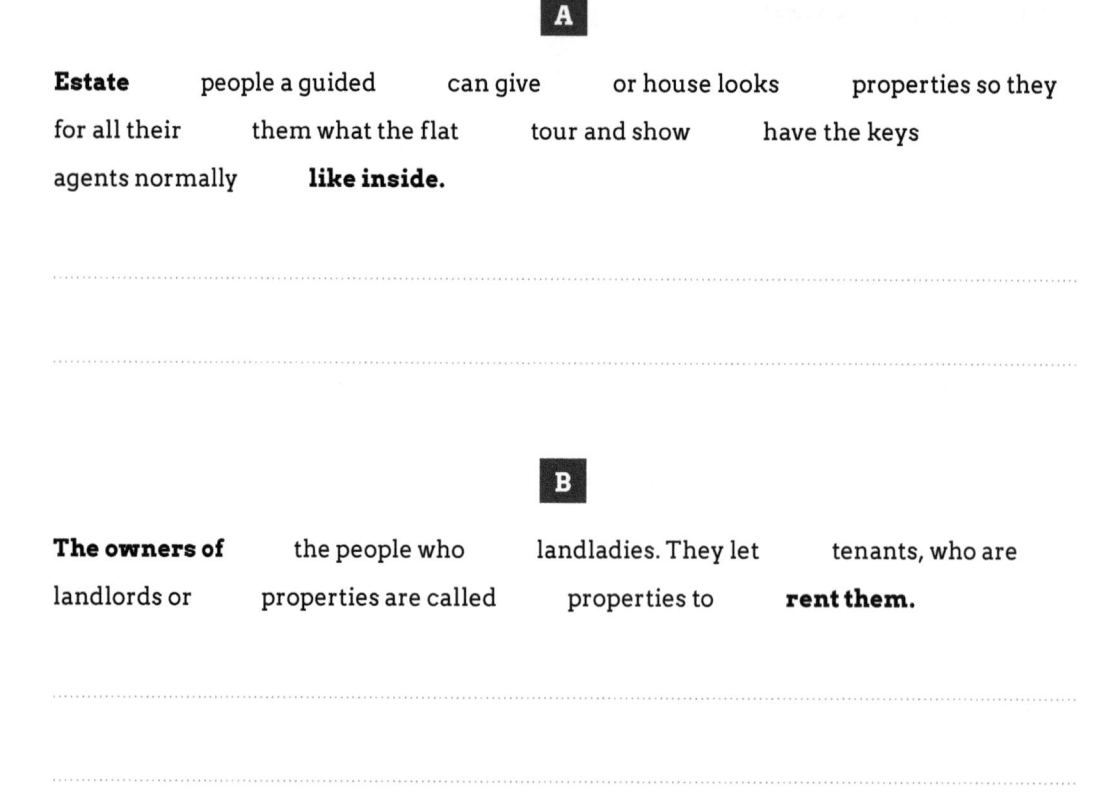

A

Estate | people a guided | can give | or house looks | properties so they
for all their | them what the flat | tour and show | have the keys
agents normally | **like inside.**

....

....

B

The owners of | the people who | landladies. They let | tenants, who are
landlords or | properties are called | properties to | **rent them.**

....

....

C

This is and houses signs outside which see why you flats **say 'to let'**.

....

....

D

Estate agents flats and houses, people buy also help to a bank and people need to go expensive, so most but property is **get a mortgage.**

....

....

E

Banks normally enough money to if they have afford the give people mortgages be able to only agree to jobs and earn **repayments.**

....

....

77. Houses

There are different types of houses in the UK. In the cities and towns many are terraced houses, but in rural areas a large number of houses are detached or semi-detached. Houses in the countryside often have gardens, but in urban areas, where there's less space, a house may only have a small back garden, or not have a garden. Houses usually have two or three floors, but there may be a basement below, or an attic above these floors. When you go through the front door, in many of them there's a room called a hall, or a corridor, which leads to the other rooms.

*Complete the text by solving the puzzles (A-E) below. The first and last pieces of each puzzle, which are in **bold**, are in the right positions, but the others aren't! Put all the pieces into the correct order and write the words on the dotted lines.*

A

On the   room and a   houses have   floor most   ground   a sitting **kitchen.**

....

....

B

There may   room and possibly   utility room,   be a separate   a downstairs bathroom   dining   **or toilet.**

....

....

C

If anyone could also works from in the house living home there **be an office.**

D

In most stairs that you upstairs on the and bathrooms are go up to a flight of floors and there's first or second houses the bedrooms **reach them.**

E

Some elderly don't have bungalows, which difficult live in find walking people who **any stairs.**

78. Furniture

When we moved into our house, we put some furniture in every room. In the kitchen and the dining room there are tables and enough chairs for our family and friends. In the sitting room we've got a large sofa, a comfortable armchair, and several chairs for people to sit on. The lamp next to the sofa gives us enough light to read, and when we're sitting down, we like to put hot and cold drinks on our coffee table. There's also a television, a bookcase and a large cupboard in the room, and a framed painting on the wall. In our bedroom, there's a double bed, with a bedside table on either side, a wardrobe, a chest of drawers and a dressing table. The children all have single beds and chests of drawers in their rooms, and we've recently put a sofa bed in the spare room.

*Complete the text by solving the puzzles (A-E) below. The first and last pieces of each puzzle, which are in **bold**, are in the right positions, but the others aren't! Put all the pieces into the correct order and write the words on the dotted lines.*

A

Most of our furniture is | shop and | ago we went | than a hundred | modern, but a few
which is more | bought some furniture | to an antique | years **years old.**

....

....

B

The side | door in the | the front | are by | stool we chose
table and the | **hall.**

....

....

HOMES 157

C

We put the office, and we bought in at the top clock on the landing the antique desk the grandfather **of the stairs.**

D

I don't often sale that's beautiful I do, I go inside shops, but when there's anything for visit antique and see whether **or interesting.**

E

If I take it afford it, I like is, and I can to buy it and think there **home.**

79. Gardens

A garden is an area of land which is next to a house, and could be at the back or front of the house, or both. Some large gardens extend to the sides of houses as well and most people have hedges, fences or walls which separate their gardens from those of their neighbours. Part of the garden usually has grass growing in it, and in some gardens vegetables and fruit are also grown. The area of grass which is cut short is called a lawn, and in other parts of the garden the grass is often allowed to grow, so it's longer and there could be a lot of weeds.

*Complete the text by solving the puzzles (A-E) below. The first and last pieces of each puzzle, which are in **bold**, are in the right positions, but the others aren't! Put all the pieces into the correct order and write the words on the dotted lines.*

A

Most   gardens which   or soil, or   flowers in their   in the earth   plants and   people grow   can be put   **in pots.**

....

....

B

Some   bad weather, and   equipment can be   protected from   where gardening   their plants are   greenhouse, where   have a   people also   others have sheds   **kept or stored.**

....

....

C

A gardener might keep a pair of gardening gloves, a spade and a fork in the shed, as well as a lawnmower, a wheelbarrow, and perhaps even **a hosepipe.**

D

Finally, a patio in the back garden is a good place to put a table and **chairs.**

E

Having a meal there or a drink or a warm enough for us to sit outside!

80. An Evening In

In the winter, when it's cold and dark, I look forward to going home after work and enjoying an evening in. When I arrive home, I switch on the lights, close the curtains and change into more comfortable clothes. I tend not to wear a sweater because we've got central heating. There are radiators in the sitting room and in our bedrooms, so most of the time it's warm and cosy. This probably explains why our gas and electricity bills are higher than they should be!

*Complete the text by solving the puzzles (A-E) below. The first and last pieces of each puzzle, which are in **bold**, are in the right positions, but the others aren't! Put all the pieces into the correct order and write the words on the dotted lines.*

A

When my | what we're going | going | home we | often we choose
to do and quite | to watch on | decide what we're | flatmates get | **TV.**

....

....

B

We sometimes | action movie | and sports | documentaries, news
we also like | or a comedy, but | film, often an | watch a | **programmes.**

....

....

C

At the | forecast so we | news we watch | to be like | the weather
end of the | weather's going | know what the | **the next day.**

....

....

D

We normally cook something at home, but at the weekend we sometimes order a home delivery pizza or an Indian **curry.**

....

....

E

We could get a take away or go out to eat because there's a restaurant near where we live, but in winter, once we get home, we usually **prefer to stay in.**

....

....

PLACES

81. Cities

Cities are important towns which tend to have much larger populations than other parts of a country. Thousands, and in many cases, millions of people live and work in these places, so they can be crowded and noisy. In fact, in excess of 50% of people in the world live in cities, and this number could increase to more than 75% in the next few decades. Many of the largest of these, including capital cities, now have skyscrapers, train stations, underground railways and airports.

Most people who live in cities take public transport or drive to work, but some choose to cycle or walk. During the rush hour there's usually a lot of traffic on the roads and there are commuters on the trains and buses. The majority of these commuters live in the suburbs or on the outskirts of the city, but visitors and tourists often stay in the city centre. There are shopping centres and department stores for those who like to go shopping, and anyone who wants to take exercise can go to a sports or leisure centre, or to one of the parks.

*Complete the text by solving the puzzles (A-E) below. The first and last pieces of each puzzle, which are in **bold**, are in the right positions, but the others aren't! Put all the pieces into the correct order and write the words on the dotted lines.*

A

Larger   during   are open   numerous museums   London, have   galleries that   and art   cities, like   **the day.**

....

....

B

These cities   can go   theatres   that you   evening as   also have   to in the   and cinemas   **well.**

....

....

C

There are plenty of food and drink and bars to from early in the morning until late at night, too, serving restaurants to choose from.

D

And if you decide to stay up late, you could go to one of the clubs and experience **the nightlife.**

E

It doesn't matter which city you visit or happen to live in, there's always something to **do!**

164 GRAMMAR PUZZLES

82. The Countryside

The countryside, or the country as it's sometimes called, is really anywhere outside urban areas, such as cities and towns. The houses and cottages in the countryside that people live in are normally in villages, on farms, or located some distance from other buildings. Some countryside is very flat, but in other areas there are hills, and even mountains and valleys. Much of the land is covered either in woods and forests, where wild animals live, or fields, where farm animals are kept and farmers grow crops. It's a great place to go for a long walk, enjoy the fresh air and see some wonderful views and scenery.

*Complete the text by solving the puzzles (A-E) below. The first and last pieces of each puzzle, which are in **bold**, are in the right positions, but the others aren't! Put all the pieces into the correct order and write the words on the dotted lines.*

A

Most   well, next   it extends to   inland, but   countryside is   the coast as   **to the sea.**

....

....

B

There   countryside, such   that are right   still water   as lakes and   of the   are areas of   in the middle   **ponds.**

....

....

C

There's moving eventually flow Streams mountains rivers, and rivers water, too. and become from hills or descend **into the sea.**

D

Life in the more relaxed quieter, more is usually than in the peaceful and countryside **cities.**

E

It's a who no longer older people retire for place to good **work.**

83. Giving Directions

We went for a long walk in the countryside on Sunday. We had a map, but after an hour or so we arrived at a village and weren't sure where to go. We decided to ask for directions. Luckily, we saw a woman who lived in the village and said she could help. This is what she told us:

"The footpath you're looking for is on the other side of the village. Turn left here and follow the road until you arrive at a country lane, just after the village shop.

*Complete the text by solving the puzzles (A-E) below. The first and last pieces of each puzzle, which are in **bold**, are in the right positions, but the others aren't! Put all the pieces into the correct order and write the words on the dotted lines.*

A

Keep walking houses on your and a few you see a pub the right, until
which bends to down the lane, **left.**

....

....

B

Go the first all the take past left over the
buildings, and **bridge.**

....

....

C

After about forks. You metres right. Follow it up goes off to the
a hundred need the road that the road **the hill.**

D

When the field on the top, walk to the farmhouse at the house and
path between you get along the **your right.**

E

You'll see where you'll there. Good find the footpath. It which is
minutes to get to your left you about ten a sign pointing
should take **luck!"**

168 GRAMMAR PUZZLES

84. The Seaside

We went to the seaside in July. The weather forecast said it would be hot for several days, so we packed our bags, put on our sunglasses and headed for the coast. The beach we went to, which has always been my favourite, is sandy, and it's never very crowded. When we arrived at ten in the morning it was already hot enough to sunbathe. We sat on the large beach towels we'd brought with us and put some suncream on to protect us from the sun. We wore hats as well.

When there's good weather and the skies are blue, the view out to sea is spectacular. Beautiful yachts and other boats of various shapes, sizes and colours move slowly across the bay. There's an island on the horizon, and you can see and hear the seagulls flying above the waves.

The sea near the beach is shallow.

*Complete the text by solving the puzzles (A-E) below. The first and last pieces of each puzzle, which are in **bold**, are in the right positions, but the others aren't! Put all the pieces into the correct order and write the words on the dotted lines.*

A

It's a lovely	summer, refreshing	games	going in to	people enjoy
warm day in	swim, and playing	temperature on a	but not cold, so	**in**
the water.				

....

....

B

| **On the** | drinks, and a hut | café that serves | creams and cold |
| sandwiches, ice | nearby where the | beach there's a | **lifeguards work.** |

....

....

C

They in any danger everyone's safe and no-one's watch what sure we're all make doing to **in the water.**

....

....

D

Next to and a number of the hut, area in front rocks the sandy left, are some and to the **of rockpools.**

....

....

E

Children go catch shrimps, which prawns, and tiny and buckets to there with nets are like small **crabs.**

....

....

170　GRAMMAR PUZZLES

85. Places to Visit in London

When tourists visit London or students come to the city to learn English, there are lots of interesting places to see. There are parks such as Richmond Park where people go to walk, cycle or see the deer that live there. Other animals can be seen at London Zoo; and for people interested in trees and plants, Kew Gardens is a good place to go to.

*Complete the text by solving the puzzles (A-E) below. The first and last pieces of each puzzle, which are in **bold**, are in the right positions, but the others aren't! Put all the pieces into the correct order and write the words on the dotted lines.*

A

The capital　　Parliament, the Tower　　and Buckingham　　Cathedral

as the Houses of　　buildings too, such　　of London, St Paul's　　historic

city has numerous　　**Palace.**

....

....

B

If you like　　National Portrait Gallery, which　　Square where you'll

particular, paintings, go　　Gallery, and the　　find the National　　to Trafalgar

art, and in　　**is nearby.**

....

....

C

There's so much to see in the museums that a visit to the British Museum or the Science Museum would be a great **idea.**

D

There are also some unusual buildings to see outside such as the London Eye, the Shard and the Elizabeth **Tower.** from the

E

You can visit all of these places by taking the city, would be a boat cruise on the River Thames, or tour through the streets of the Tube, but going on an open top bus **more fun!**

TRAVEL

86. Planes and Flying

Planes (the long word is aeroplanes) are very large vehicles with wings and several engines. They're extremely heavy, but their engines are powerful enough to lift them off the ground. A plane starts every journey on a runway, which is like a road next to an airport. From a stationary position it starts to move forward, before it accelerates and travels along the runway at great speed. Then, in no time at all, it leaves the ground, goes up in the air, and into the sky. When this happens, we say the plane is taking off.

Before take-off, the captain welcomes all the passengers (the people travelling on the plane), and tells them about the flight and the weather. When the plane is ready to fly, there's a safety demonstration, and the crew check that everyone has put on their seatbelts (which have to be worn on a plane for safety reasons). A few minutes after the plane has gone up in the air, the passengers can undo their seatbelts to move about. They can relax and have something to eat and drink. They may also listen to music, watch a film, play games or read. Business people can do some work if they want to.

*Complete the text by solving the puzzles (A-E) below. The first and last pieces of each puzzle, which are in **bold**, are in the right positions, but the others aren't! Put all the pieces into the correct order and write the words on the dotted lines.*

A

The passengers   journey is almost   when the   seatbelts again   on their   put   **over.**

....

....

B

The plane then   land. When   towards the   say the plane   flies down   this happens we   **is landing.**

....

....

TRAVEL 173

C

Once it's on runway until again, it moves the ground it gets slowly along the **to the airport.**

D

Soon after it airline and wishes for choosing country they've just thanks everyone stops, the captain stay in the city or them a pleasant to fly with the **arrived in.**

E

The passengers off the seatbelts, take plane and walk luggage, get their hand then undo their **into the airport.**

87. Airports

If you're going to take a flight (a journey by air), to a city in another country, you'll need a ticket, which you can buy online, and your passport. The day you fly you should try to get to the airport early with all the information that's required, including your flight details. Make sure you pack everything you're going to need when you get to your destination and know exactly what you have in your bags. At airports you have to go through customs on both departure and arrival. Everything that leaves and is brought into the country is checked.

*Complete the text by solving the puzzles (A-E) below. The first and last pieces of each puzzle, which are in **bold**, are in the right positions, but the others aren't! Put all the pieces into the correct order and write the words on the dotted lines.*

A

Once you've | right terminal, | you information | and found the | screens which give | at the airport | check the | arrived | **about your flight.**

....

....

B

They tell | to go to when | delayed. They | board your | time or | flight is on | it's time to | which gate | you if your | also tell you | **plane.**

....

....

C

It's a good idea | for the airline | who's working | as you arrive. When
bags to the person | and give your | in as soon | show your ticket
you check in, you | to check | **you're flying with.**

D

You're allowed | bags. These are placed | to take hand | larger cases and
your seat, but not | the lockers above | and put it in | luggage with you
in the hold.

E

As soon as | lounge. Have | departure | you can | you've checked in
a good | go to the | **flight!**

88. Boats

Boats are vehicles that travel on water, and there are many different types of boat. Large boats are called ships, and some of these ships carry passengers across oceans and seas. Boats that travel shorter distances, known as ferries, transport people along rivers, or from one country or island to another nearby. Ferries, for example, travel across the Channel between England and France, a journey that usually takes less than a day, and between England and Spain, normally an overnight crossing. There are cruise ships which go round the world, stopping at different ports so people can see and visit interesting places during the cruise. On voyages which take days or weeks, passengers have cabins so they can sleep at night, and they sit on seats or at tables during the day. Most of these ships have shops, bars and restaurants, and on some there are cinemas, casinos and swimming pools.

*Complete the text by solving the puzzles (A-E) below. The first and last pieces of each puzzle, which are in **bold**, are in the right positions, but the others aren't! Put all the pieces into the correct order and write the words on the dotted lines.*

A

| **The floors** | large windows and | and there are | called decks | ships are |
| balconies on | or levels on | **upper decks.** | | |

....

....

B

| **Some of the** | countries to be | ships, which take | and heaviest |
| bought and | goods to other | ships are cargo | largest | **sold.** |

....

....

C

Many of containers to keep is kept in products in vast these transport refrigerated containers, and food **it fresh.**

D

Other boats rescue people on fishing smaller than we eat, and lifeboats the fish and seafood who are in trouble boats to catch ships. We rely are much **at sea.**

E

Boats are on our lakes too. There are boats to travel people on holiday hire and at sea, and and for leisure used for sport on our rivers, yachts rowing boats **along our canals.**

178 GRAMMAR PUZZLES

89. Holidays

People go on holiday throughout the year, but summer holidays are more popular than holidays in the winter. During the summer months they travel to places where they can enjoy warm weather and sunshine. The weather in the UK can be warm and sunny, but it can also be cold, cloudy and wet, so people go abroad to countries like France, Spain, Italy and Greece. They stay in hotels, apartments, and campsites and spend much of the day at the seaside. They sunbathe on the beach, go swimming in the sea, or might choose one of the sports or activities available. Sailing, surfing, diving, hiring boats, water-skiing and walking along the coast are all popular activities.

*Complete the text by solving the puzzles (A-E) below. The first and last pieces of each puzzle, which are in **bold**, are in the right positions, but the others aren't! Put all the pieces into the correct order and write the words on the dotted lines.*

A

Some people	in the winter	beach holidays. Skiing	to ski in Europe
popular places	holidays to	prefer skiing	of the most	holidays are
months, and one	**is the Alps.**

....

....

B

| **These are** | Germany, France and | countries, including | eight different |
| huge area in | mountains that | Austria, Switzerland, | cover a | **Italy.** |

....

....

C

People skiing is good snow for weather, and to have good skiing also hope who go **important.**

D

Skiers holiday them on cold on clothes with can be very take warm because it **the slopes.**

E

When they everything else helmets and normally hire skis, sticks, boots, ski resort they they need, including arrive at their **goggles.**

90. Sightseeing and Tourism

If you don't want to go on holiday to lie on a beach or ski down a mountain, you could travel to a country you've never been to before. There are so many things to see and experience when you become a tourist. You can stay in an old city and go sightseeing, or travel across a country and enjoy its beautiful scenery. If you choose to do some sightseeing, a good place to start is the nearest tourist office. The brochures there are normally available free of charge. You may have to pay for a guidebook, but it will tell you where everything is and you won't get lost. See the sights you've read or been told are worth seeing. You can visit historic places like cathedrals and castles, or walk around an art gallery. If it's a sunny day and you'd rather be outside, why not go to one of the busy markets? Buy some souvenirs to take home to your family and friends.

*Complete the text by solving the puzzles (A-E) below. The first and last pieces of each puzzle, which are in **bold**, are in the right positions, but the others aren't! Put all the pieces into the correct order and write the words on the dotted lines.*

A

Take photos	on a tour of	the fountains. Walk	and the squares,
of the parks or go	of the buildings	through one	the statues and
the city.			

B

| **In the** | tired, or go | or your hotel | the nightlife if | stay in your apartment |
| evening you can | out and enjoy | if you're | **you're not!** | |

C

Try some of restaurants, bars cities, there's food and of the local a choice of hundreds drink. In big **and nightclubs.**

D

You film, or to see a to watch cinema to the the theatre could go **a play.**

E

If you concert. Whatever to a a great music, go like you do, have **time!**

TRANSPORT

91. Learning to Drive

Driving a car is a skill that people need if they want to get a driving licence and drive safely on the roads. The best way to learn is to have driving lessons with a qualified driving instructor. They sit beside you in the passenger's seat and explain what you have to do. You can choose to learn in a car with manual gears, which are operated and controlled by hand, or if you prefer you can learn in an automatic car. Automatic cars have a number of gears, including P for park, R for reverse, N for neutral and D for drive. Learner drivers, however, are advised to learn in a car with manual gears. This is because, in the UK, if you pass your test in a manual car you can also drive an automatic car. If, however, you learn to drive in an automatic car you won't be allowed to drive a car with manual gears.

*Complete the text by solving the puzzles (A-E) below. The first and last pieces of each puzzle, which are in **bold**, are in the right positions, but the others aren't! Put all the pieces into the correct order and write the words on the dotted lines.*

A

There are important is the well, and one learn as need to things you many other expression "mirror, of the most **signal, manoeuvre".**

....

....

B

Before you look in your you should always another road right into a roundabout, or drive around turn left or **mirrors first.**

....

....

C

Then indicator so other signal, with your what you're pedestrians know you indicate, or drivers and **about to do.**

D

Finally, you sounds difficult, don't means you change position. If this direction or your manoeuvre, which your speed, your **worry!**

E

Your driving practise it again you need to enough, to pass you drive well be able to teach everything instructor will enough, and safely and again until know, and you'll **your test.**

92. Gears and Pedals

Gears are controls that make cars move. If you want to drive in a car with manual gears, one of the important things to learn is how to change gear. When you start the engine, the car is in neutral gear which means the engine isn't moving the wheels. You move from neutral to first gear to move the wheels forwards, but if you want to go backwards, you move from neutral to reverse gear.

When the car's moving forwards, and as it goes faster, you move up the gears from first, to second, then third, fourth, fifth, and in most cars, sixth gear. Fifth and sixth gear are normally used when a car is being driven at higher speeds on main roads and motorways. When you want to slow down you move down from fifth or sixth to a lower gear. Change gear from the lower gear to neutral again just before you stop or park.

There are three pedals which you operate with your feet. The one on the left is called the clutch.

*Complete the text by solving the puzzles (A-E) below. The first and last pieces of each puzzle, which are in **bold**, are in the right positions, but the others aren't! Put all the pieces into the correct order and write the words on the dotted lines.*

A

When you | change gear. This | find it gets | your foot, you can
enough will | the clutch with | practise it | drivers who | press down on
at first but | is difficult | **easier.**

....

....

B

The pedal | the brake. This | down and | middle is | slow
helps you | in the | **stop.**

....

C

To stop if you've parked put on the properly you the car handbrake, especially also need to **on a slope.**

D

The pedal on the accelerator, which or reduce the right is increase is used to **speed.**

E

There are many the pedals and about driving, but need to learn else should be how to use other things you change gear, everything once you know **easier!**

93. Public Transport

In cities like London, millions of people travel from one place to another every day. Without public transport there would be far too many cars on the roads. There would be traffic jams everywhere. Public transport for many people is the quickest, cheapest and most convenient way of travelling in a city. The underground railway in London opened in 1863. It's known as the Tube and has trains on different lines which cross the city in every direction.

*Complete the text by solving the puzzles (A-E) below. The first and last pieces of each puzzle, which are in **bold**, are in the right positions, but the others aren't! Put all the pieces into the correct order and write the words on the dotted lines.*

A

Three   line and the   Northern   and most famous   line, the District   are the   busiest   of the   **Central line.**

....

....

B

The stations   lifts and stairs move   actually above   a train to work   level to another   the lines are   and many of   so they can catch   people from one   the ground. Escalators,   **or to go home.**

....

....

C

Buses also can enjoy views one, where people and an upper London many of have two levels, a every direction. In cross the city in lower deck them are red and **of the city.**

D

They take unless you're in way to travel are a good of the traffic, but destination because reach their longer to **a hurry.**

E

There can hire bikes, that people can travel by even public are cars, and river, so they too, and there's transport on the **boat.**

188 GRAMMAR PUZZLES

94. Coaches and Trains

People who want to travel from one city or town to another may choose to drive. Long journeys, however, can be exhausting and not everyone has a car or can afford to pay for the petrol. For people without much money, travelling by coach is a good option. It's normally cheaper than driving or going by train, and coaches travel to most towns and cities, where many of them end up at a coach station. Victoria Coach Station in London is a well-known destination. Coaches arrive here from, and travel to, a large number of other places in the UK, and some parts of Europe.

*Complete the text by solving the puzzles (A-E) below. The first and last pieces of each puzzle, which are in **bold**, are in the right positions, but the others aren't! Put all the pieces into the correct order and write the words on the dotted lines.*

A

Coaches are   travel within cities   also faster than   comfortable than

than between   buses tend to   usually more   buses, partly because

and towns, rather   buses. They're   **them.**

....

....

B

Trains can   than by any other   apart from a plane   it's often quicker

of transport, and   and enjoyable form   form of transport,   to go by train

be a relaxing   **or a helicopter!**

....

....

C

Trains travel | are also called | the east. They're made | country from the
of carriages which | the west to | across the | up of a number | south and
north to the | **coaches.**

D

Most of the | food and drinks | buffet carriage where | passengers to sit
are small restaurants | and on some there | usually at least one
carriages are for | can be bought, | in, but there's | **as well.**

E

One disadvantage, though, | on a coach or | to travel by | costs much
with friends normally | very expensive | is that it can be | sharing a car
train. Going by road | **less.**

95. Safety on the Roads

Anyone thinking of riding a motorbike or cycling should realise how dangerous it can be. Cars, vans and lorries share the roads with motorbikes and bikes. Motorcyclists and cyclists are injured or killed every week when they're hit by larger vehicles and knocked off their bikes. Governments try to make people aware of the dangers and improve safety, but it's still a tragic situation. Wearing a helmet to protect their heads is essential, and anyone on a motorbike or a bike, or driving a car, should take extra care. They ought to check their mirrors to see whether any other vehicles are near them, and must do this before they turn left or right, or join another road.

The other people who need to be careful, especially when they cross the road, are pedestrians. Trying to cross a road where motorists don't expect it can be very dangerous. Pedestrians should use pedestrian crossings, and only cross the road when the traffic lights turn green.

*Complete the text by solving the puzzles (A-E) below. The first and last pieces of each puzzle, which are in **bold**, are in the right positions, but the others aren't! Put all the pieces into the correct order and write the words on the dotted lines.*

A

If there's a	as they can get	emergency services	UK, call 999 as soon
scene as soon	anywhere in the	arrive at the	as possible. The
serious accident	**there.**		

....

....

B

| **They're able** | traffic on the | accidents quite | there's a lot of | at most |
| even when | to arrive | quickly, | **roads.** | |

....

....

C

This is and flashing speed, but of their sirens driven at high their vehicles are not only because also because **lights.**

D

When other road so an ambulance, a try to move over a siren or see engine can go their mirrors, they cars hear people in police car or a fire to the side of the flashing lights in **past them.**

E

The emergency help people drive across thousands been in an our towns and year when they who have countryside to of lives every services save **accident.**

SAFETY AND SECURITY

96. Medical Emergencies

You should always get help as soon as possible in an emergency. In the UK you do this by calling 999 and speaking to the emergency services. You'll be able to tell them whether you need the fire service, the police, or an ambulance. If it's a serious medical problem, they'll send paramedics to you in an ambulance. Call 999 at once if someone has serious chest pain and could be having a heart attack or a stroke. Call them as well if a person is unconscious, has stopped breathing or is finding it difficult to breathe. Their lips might be going blue. If they've eaten or drunk something which you think is poisonous, call 999. If they've got a deep cut and are bleeding heavily, a bad eye injury, or a serious burn, call 999. If you're not sure what needs to be done, try to stay calm and ask the emergency services. They'll tell you what to do on the phone, and may explain how to put someone into the recovery position if they've lost consciousness but are still breathing. They can do this while you wait for the paramedics to arrive.

*Complete the text by solving the puzzles (A-E) below. The first and last pieces of each puzzle, which are in **bold**, are in the right positions, but the others aren't! Put all the pieces into the correct order and write the words on the dotted lines.*

A

In less serious | feel very well | isn't an emergency | or has had a minor
but someone doesn't | situations where it | **accident, call 111.**

B

You may be | a first aid training | the person first | you've been on
aid, especially if | able to give | **course.**

C

Even if you haven't been | first aid that could help you | are first aid kits and guides to basic | deal with the **problem.** | trained, there

D

If you've of these | insect bite got one | should be able | with an **or a sting.** | guides, you | to help

E

A bruise, a minor well, as can a **help.** | injury, but if you can be treated as | minor sports think it's a broken | bone, get medical burn, or a cut

97. Safety at Home

To avoid injuries, keep rooms and stairs free of clutter, especially on the floor. If objects are left on the floor, people can easily trip and fall. Any water on the floor should be cleaned up at once, so people don't slip and hurt themselves. If a glass object breaks, use a dustpan and brush or a vacuum cleaner to remove any broken glass, so people don't cut their hands. Glass left on the floor could result in serious injury; anyone with bare feet could cut themselves badly. If you're doing gardening or DIY, use the right equipment and wear the right clothing and shoes. Never do a job which you don't have the skills or experience to do safely. Be very careful with ladders, lawnmowers and gardening tools.

To prevent a fire, use a smoke alarm and test it regularly. Fires can spread quickly, so everyone must know how to get out of a building as soon as possible. All gas and electric heaters should be checked regularly and replaced when they're old. Don't use flexes that are damaged or put too many plugs into one electrical socket – you could cause a fire.

*Complete the text by solving the puzzles (A-E) below. The first and last pieces of each puzzle, which are in **bold**, are in the right positions, but the others aren't! Put all the pieces into the correct order and write the words on the dotted lines.*

A

Keep appliances, such   and curtains   all heating   clothes, furniture away from   **as cookers.**

....

....

B

Be very they're lit and   matches. An   the room when   lighters and always be in   candles, cigarettes,   careful with   adult should   **put out.**

....

....

C

Finally, never into the take one hands or touch electrical with wet appliances **bathroom.**

....

....

D

Water electricity, could kill electrocuted conducts and being **someone.**

....

....

E

Your safest world. Make be the home place in the should **sure it is.**

....

....

98. Looking after Children

Kitchens can be dangerous places for small children. If you're cooking, whenever possible, use the hotplates at the back of a hob, or the gas rings at the back of a stove. Place pan handles away from the front of the cooker so children can't reach them. Kettles should also be out of reach. Don't put hot drinks near the edge of a table, put them nearer the middle, so children can't knock them over. Keep sharp objects such as knives in drawers and always make sure children are a safe distance away when they're being used. Plastic bags should be kept away from babies and toddlers as well, because of the risk of suffocation. Cupboards which can only be reached by adults and can be locked would be a good place to keep them. It's important to be careful in the bathroom, too. Small children should not be left on their own when they're having a bath or near the hot water tap. Fill the bath with cold water, then carefully with hot water, and always check the temperature before a child gets into it.

*Complete the text by solving the puzzles (A-E) below. The first and last pieces of each puzzle, which are in **bold**, are in the right positions, but the others aren't! Put all the pieces into the correct order and write the words on the dotted lines.*

A

Medicines and | from children to | chemicals should | household or garden
burning their | or small children | prevent babies | be kept away
swallowing them or | **skin.**

....

....

B

Gardening | reach, locked | also be stored | tools should
lawnmowers, and sharp | shed if you | in a garden | out of children's
equipment, like | **have one.**

....

....

SAFETY AND SECURITY 197

C

Make any equipment a safe distance when it's being children are
away from sure **used.**

....

....

D

Whenever keep children or fireworks, a bonfire, barbecue,
there's a **well away.**

....

....

E

If you're as close to and keep them or across or near
the pavement, however, children's hands walking on a road, hold small
you as possible.

....

....

99. Preventing Burglaries

A large number of burglaries are committed when burglars get into properties through unlocked doors or windows. It's best to make sure all your doors and windows have proper locks and are locked every time you go out. Front and back doors should be strong, at least four centimetres thick, and have a deadlock, a type of lock that needs a key to open or close it. A burglar alarm will also help prevent a break-in. Ensure the sign for your alarm is in a visible place on the wall near the front door. This alone is likely to deter anyone thinking of breaking in. Put all your valuables in a safe place in your property, either locked away or somewhere they can't easily be found. Don't put them anywhere they can be seen through a window. When you're out, it's a good idea to leave a light on in one of the rooms because it will make people think there's someone at home.

*Complete the text by solving the puzzles (A-E) below. The first and last pieces of each puzzle, which are in **bold**, are in the right positions, but the others aren't! Put all the pieces into the correct order and write the words on the dotted lines.*

A

If you're going   an answering   never leave this   don't know
other reason, don't   a holiday or some   away for   information on
well, and   tell anyone you   **machine.**

....

....

B

Burglars often   if they're at   people's   them to see   find out
and call   numbers   **home.**

....

....

SAFETY AND SECURITY 199

C

A fence trouble climbing getting into for them to have
a burglar from be high enough but it needs to can help prevent
your back garden, **over it.**

D

Put locks of pounds, and well, because valuable of garden sheds
are kept cars worth thousands, hundreds and garages as on the doors
objects worth **there.**

E

Being part be sure whether watch scheme take a
they wouldn't normally bite them, but burglar can't as can a dog. A
a dog will can also help, of a neighbourhood **chance!**

200 GRAMMAR PUZZLES

100. Pedestrians and Cyclists

Pedestrians should always find the safest places to walk and to cross a road. On busy or main roads, they're advised to use subways or footbridges wherever possible. On pedestrian crossings it's important to wait until the lights turn green. If there's a traffic island in the middle, they should treat the two roads as two different crossings. Otherwise, they could choose a place to cross where they can see clearly in all directions. They must make sure, though, that motorists, motorcyclists and cyclists can see them too. Before they cross, they should remember to look left, look right and then left again. Traffic can often be heard before it's seen, so it's a good idea for pedestrians to listen carefully as well.

*Complete the text by solving the puzzles (A-E) below. The first and last pieces of each puzzle, which are in **bold**, are in the right positions, but the others aren't! Put all the pieces into the correct order and write the words on the dotted lines.*

A

| **Cyclists** | distance between | they wear | all other | keep a safe |
| themselves and | helmets and | safer if | are much | **vehicles.** |

....

....

B

| **It's** | other | them to | inside of | on the | dangerous for |
| overtake | **vehicles.** |

....

....

C

In the cars which are when they try left, and don't accidents happen about to turn of the worst lorries or UK, some to cycle past **see them.**

D

They should them during coloured clothing visibility, and dark or drivers see when it's always use lights that helps wear brightly there's poor **the day.**

E

Finally, they tell them and signs a serious light can cause traffic lights do what must through a red to do. Going **accident.**

ANIMALS

101. The Animal Family

I was amazed to discover that rabbits, squirrels, mice and rats are some of our closest relatives! Once I found out, I wondered whether other mammals were related to each other as well. When I looked at pictures of deer, camels and giraffes, it occurred to me that they might be close relatives. They're different sizes, but they all have long, thin necks and legs, and their faces are quite similar, so I wasn't surprised to find out that they were. I was, though, very surprised to discover cows and pigs happen to be related to whales and dolphins!

While we're on the subject of mammals, have you ever looked at a photo of a seal and been reminded of any other animals? Their bodies are different, but when I look at a seal's face I can't help thinking of dogs with similar faces, eyes and whiskers, and in particular, black labradors.

*Complete the text by solving the puzzles (A-E) below. The first and last pieces of each puzzle, which are in **bold**, are in the right positions, but the others aren't! Put all the pieces into the correct order and write the words on the dotted lines.*

A

They   years   and dogs are   gone their   ago, but seals   may have   million   separate ways 50   **related too.**

....

....

B

Female   them with   birth to   and feed   mammals give   their babies   **their milk.**

....

....

C

This and reptiles   all of which   and tortoises,   from birds,
makes them   snakes   such as crocodiles,   different   **lay eggs.**

D

Mammals   exception, they   from birds   with one   because,
different   are also   **can't fly.**

E

Can you   only flying   to the question is   mammal that   mammals on
bats, the   The answer   think of a   can fly?   has wings and   **Earth!**

102. How Animals Look

Animals are amazing creatures. No wonder there are so many wildlife programmes. It's fascinating to see how they behave in the wild and what they look like. There's great variety in their shapes and sizes, from the largest whale or elephant to the smallest mouse. Crocodiles, sharks and snakes look prehistoric and dangerous, which is probably because they are! Others that don't look dangerous at all can be very dangerous: chimpanzees and poisonous frogs, for example. Some animals have beautiful patterns on their bodies. Tigers and zebras, for instance, have stripes, and cheetahs and leopards have spots.

Many of the birds, reptiles, amphibians and fish on our planet are very colourful. Two of the most colourful types of bird are parrots and flamingos; and frogs, butterflies and lizards are all sorts of different colours. The chameleon, a type of lizard, can even change the colours on its own body!

*Complete the text by solving the puzzles (A-E) below. The first and last pieces of each puzzle, which are in **bold**, are in the right positions, but the others aren't! Put all the pieces into the correct order and write the words on the dotted lines.*

A

Mammals like | white, brown, grey, | colourful, with | be less
usually black, | cats tend to | fur that's | dogs and | **ginger or yellow.**

B

One | a large | colourful, though, is | which is | mandrill,
that's extremely | the male | **monkey.**

C

Charles was the most the naturalist mammal in believed it
Darwin, colourful and biologist, **the world.**

....

....

D

It has dark is bright fur and its pink and green or grey bottom
blue.

....

....

E

It also and a yellow or long, red nose, blue face, has a a bright
orange beard!

....

....

103. How Animals Move

Animals' bodies, and where they live, have a lot to do with how they move. Snakes slither along the ground because they haven't got any legs. Lizards and other reptiles crawl on four legs and so do frogs and toads. Insects crawl too, if they can't fly, or when they aren't flying. Most birds fly because they have wings, and bats fly as well, as do insects with wings, like wasps, bees and flies. Almost all animals move forwards, whether they're in the air or on land, but crabs have legs which are better at moving them sideways, so that's what they do!

Fish, dolphins and whales swim because they live in water and their bodies have evolved to move in water. Animals that live on land and in rivers or the sea can also swim, like crocodiles and penguins. Monkeys, squirrels and koala bears live in trees, so they know how to climb (and some monkeys swing from tree to tree if they need to move fast). Mountain goats and tree frogs can climb too. Their names tell us where they go climbing!

*Complete the text by solving the puzzles (A-E) below. The first and last pieces of each puzzle, which are in **bold**, are in the right positions, but the others aren't! Put all the pieces into the correct order and write the words on the dotted lines.*

A

Frogs   mammals like   and so do   jump,   grasshoppers, and   hop and   insects like   and toads   **kangaroos.**

....

....

B

Most   cheetahs   legs can   run at great   four   animals with   some, like   and lions, can   run, and   **speed.**

....

....

C

Horses | rather than | normally say | quickly as | they gallop
run very | well, but we | **run.**

D

Of | we can | only have | beings | legs, and | course, human
two | **run too.**

E

There's | can. It's called | two legs, | faster than we | much | can run
bird with | though, that | a large | **an ostrich!**

104. How Animals Sound

There are words in the English language for many of the sounds that animals make. The ones we use the most are made by our pets, or animals that live near us or on farms. Dogs bark when they're excited and growl when they're being aggressive. Cats meow when they want something and purr when they're happy. Horses neigh and donkeys bray. Cows moo and sheep bleat and baa. Pigs grunt, ducks quack, cocks crow and hens cluck. Most pets and animals on farms make some sort of sound. Even mice do. If you listen very carefully when you see a mouse, you may hear it squeak.

*Complete the text by solving the puzzles (A-E) below. The first and last pieces of each puzzle, which are in **bold**, are in the right positions, but the others aren't! Put all the pieces into the correct order and write the words on the dotted lines.*

A

Wild continents make also other Africa and animals in **sounds.**

....

....

B

People the sounds they hear these some of on safaris make at night who go the day, but animals during **are amazing.**

....

....

ANIMALS 209

C

Birds sing, and lions and twitter. chatter whistle, tweet Monkeys **roar.**

....

....

D

Elephants hiss. Even insects and wild dogs make sounds. Bees trumpet, wolves croak and snakes howl, frogs **and flies buzz.**

....

....

E

In hot before they often hear sound of crickets noises at countries one mosquitos whine of the loudest chirping and we night is the **bite us!**

....

....

105. World Records

The world is a much more interesting place because we share it with so many extraordinary animals. Animals, of course, are very different from us, but some of them are extraordinary even compared to other animals. There are many ways of describing these animals in the English language, and a type of adjective called a superlative is often used. 'The largest', for example, is one of these adjectives. Blue whales are the largest and the heaviest creatures in our oceans, and the largest and heaviest creatures on land are African elephants.

Many other amazing animals are also native to the continent of Africa. Giraffes, for instance, are the tallest animals in the world, with the longest legs and necks, and ostriches are the largest and heaviest birds.

*Complete the text by solving the puzzles (A-E) below. The first and last pieces of each puzzle, which are in **bold**, are in the right positions, but the others aren't! Put all the pieces into the correct order and write the words on the dotted lines.*

A

The peregrine world creature called a in the fastest is a bird **falcon.**

....

....

B

These which stands hour, or 200 mph, known to fly for 'miles per kilometres per been faster than 320 birds have **hour'.**

....

....

C

The fastest land animals are cheetahs, which can run at a speed of more than 96 kph, or 60 mph, and some of the slowest are **tortoises.**

D

These animals, though, have also lived the longest. In 1770 a British explorer called Captain Cook gave a tortoise to the Tongan **royal family.**

E

It was alive in three centuries and died in 1965 at the age of at least 188. It was one of the oldest animals that has **ever lived.**

NATURE

106. Safaris, Zoos, and Farms

If you want to see wild animals in their natural habitat, one of the best places to visit is Africa. In most countries there are zoos, but the game reserves in African countries like Kenya and South Africa are much bigger than zoos, and the animals live freely in their natural environment. When they go on a safari to Africa, people usually want to see lions, leopards, buffaloes, elephants and rhinos. These animals are known as the 'big five', not because of their size, but because in the past they were the most difficult and dangerous to hunt on foot. Although nowadays the 'big five' are protected in most reserves and should hopefully survive, the situation is very different elsewhere in Africa and other parts of the world. Poaching and the destruction of their environment have become serious problems for all five, and rhinos in particular are in danger of becoming extinct.

*Complete the text by solving the puzzles (A-E) below. The first and last pieces of each puzzle, which are in **bold**, are in the right positions, but the others aren't! Put all the pieces into the correct order and write the words on the dotted lines.*

A

For most   places we   TV or in   only   animals are on   of us, the see wild   **a zoo.**

....

....

B

Animals in zoos   which people   enclosures so   in conditions   cages or escape, often   are kept in   they can't   **consider cruel.**

....

....

C

Other animals are farms have or need of years these kept on farms, what we want and for hundreds with much of provided us **in our daily lives.**

D

We get lamb all come from hens, and products from our dairy chicken and goats, our eggs sheep. Beef, pork, our wool from cows and **from farms.**

E

While animal difference in the issue for farm to make a real still a serious farming has begun welfare is animals, organic **UK.**

107. Cats and Dogs

The only animals which are tame, rather than wild, are the ones that live with us at home as pets. Cats and dogs are the most popular pets in the world, and have been our companions for thousands of years. We become so fond of them that for many of us they're part of the family. Physically, cats and dogs are quite similar. Most of them have fur which covers their bodies. They all have four legs, paws with claws, tails, and warm, wet noses, but cats and dogs have very different personalities.

Cats are independent animals. Their territory is important to them. They like to decide when and where to spend time with people. This may explain why they don't like being picked up, carried, and forced to sit on someone's lap.

Dogs are normally sociable animals. Since the time they hunted in packs they've always wanted to be with other dogs or humans. Most dogs like people moving towards them, patting them and playing with them. They need more attention and exercise than cats. Dogs enjoy going for regular walks with their owners, but cats have no interest in doing this. Unlike dogs, they're happy to be left at home during the day.

Cats and dogs tend to play different games.

*Complete the text by solving the puzzles (A-E) below. The first and last pieces of each puzzle, which are in **bold**, are in the right positions, but the others aren't! Put all the pieces into the correct order and write the words on the dotted lines.*

A

Cats quite often   a piece of   to the end of   attached   objects, they're   small moving   especially if   jump on   **string.**

B

Dogs   them. They run   objects you've   them up in their   fast as they after them as   thrown for   like to fetch   can and pick   **mouths.**

C

When some dogs ... out of their mouths ...

(scrambled words: When / some dogs / out of their / them back, / drop the objects in / you. Others / to pull them / they bring / challenge you / front of / **mouths.**)

D

Dogs are ... much ... **basic commands.**

(scrambled words: Dogs are / much / learn to obey / basic commands. / cats, they / than cats. Unlike / easier to train)

E

If you ... something, ... **ignores you.**

(scrambled words: If you / something, / tell a cat to do / sits. If you / dog to 'sit', it / it usually / tell a trained / **ignores you.**)

216　GRAMMAR PUZZLES

108. Birds

Scientists believe birds are descended from dinosaurs, those huge prehistoric animals which are now extinct, which means they no longer exist. They probably survived because, unlike dinosaurs, they had wings and could fly.

You may have seen birds flying together in flocks, which many of them do, and some travel thousands of miles when they migrate. Although most birds can fly, some larger birds can't. Ostriches and emus can't fly, but they can run very fast. An ostrich has been known to run faster than a horse. Penguins can't fly either, but they can swim. When they're swimming in water, they move their wings like other birds when they're flying!

Birds have feathers, two wings and two legs. They also have a beak and warm blood, but they don't have any teeth. Some species are very colourful. Flamingos are bright pink and parrots are green, yellow, red and blue. Parrots are intelligent and can be very amusing, especially when they repeat words and phrases that humans say. Most birds are also sociable, spending much of their time with other birds, singing and calling each other and using visual signals to communicate. The songs of male nightingales are some of the most beautiful sounds in nature.

*Complete the text by solving the puzzles (A-E) below. The first and last pieces of each puzzle, which are in **bold**, are in the right positions, but the others aren't! Put all the pieces into the correct order and write the words on the dotted lines.*

A

People　　their kitchen　　gardens so they　　birds from　　tables in their　　put bird　　can watch　　**windows.**

....

....

B

They　　in the　　water, especially　　food and　　them　　give　　**winter.**

....

....

C

Birdwatching | creatures, but | because they're | hobby. We love
they need to | to watch birds | is a popular | beautiful and amazing
be protected.

D

There are | according | birds in the | many as 18,000 | species of
there may be as | at least 10,000 | world, and | **to some reports.**

E

A large | danger of | however, probably | these species, | number of
a thousand, are in | well over | **extinction.**

109. Insects

Insects are much smaller than animals and birds. They've got six legs and their bodies are divided into three sections. They've also got long, thin parts on their heads, called antennae, which they use to touch and feel things. Most insects have wings and can fly, but some move around by walking as well, and others can even swim.

Insects can be annoying, and some are dangerous. Mosquitos are very common in hot countries. They bite humans and animals and drink their blood. When they do this our skin becomes itchy and uncomfortable. Prevent this by wearing long sleeves and trousers. There are sprays that mosquitos don't like and creams you can use to stop the itching. Some flies bite as well, and horsefly bites are very unpleasant. Flies are dirty and, like mosquitos, they can spread diseases. If you ever eat outside on a hot day, make sure they don't land on your plate or your food.

*Complete the text by solving the puzzles (A-E) below. The first and last pieces of each puzzle, which are in **bold**, are in the right positions, but the others aren't! Put all the pieces into the correct order and write the words on the dotted lines.*

A

Wasps like   sting you,   us too. They   if they   irritating, and   to fly around   can be   **it's painful.**

....

....

B

Some   use pesticides to   their crops. This   problems for   locusts, cause   control and kill   they damage   insects, like   is why farmers   farmers because   **them.**

....

....

C

Other | and they'll stay | some mothballs | moths, damage
and wardrobes | our clothes. Put | insects, called | in your drawers | **away.**

D

Not all insects | have wings that | some are | though, and | are a problem,
are beautiful | wonderful. Butterflies | **colours.**

E

Bees | shirts and | produce silk | with honey, | to make ties,
provide us | which is used | type of moth, | and silkworms, a | **dresses.**

110. Plants

A plant grows in the earth. Its roots spread outwards and downwards. They support the plant and give it water. All plants need water and light to grow. The part of the plant which grows above the earth is called the stem. Once the stem has grown, the plant can produce leaves and flowers.

Trees are the largest plants in the world. The stem of a tree is called a trunk. Branches grow on the trunk and leaves grow on the branches. Some trees are evergreen, which means they keep their leaves and they stay green through the different seasons. Other trees are deciduous. This means their leaves fall off in the autumn and new ones grow the following spring.

Plants are very important for human beings and animals. They remove harmful carbon dioxide from the air and turn it into oxygen, which prevents global warming. We depend on them for food, especially for fruit and vegetables.

*Complete the text by solving the puzzles (A-E) below. The first and last pieces of each puzzle, which are in **bold**, are in the right positions, but the others aren't! Put all the pieces into the correct order and write the words on the dotted lines.*

A

We wouldn't | get a lot of | plants, including | plants, and we
coffee without | our medicines from | like tea or | have drinks | **aspirin.**

B

Many of the | rubber, for | from plants. Anything | in shops come
products we buy | plastic or | made of | **example.**

C

Soap, shampoo, plants, and what from cotton are we get from
our clothes made paint and all about the wood also from **trees?**

D

Wood is well as thousands boats, furniture buildings and
and cardboard, as used to make and fences, paper **of other things.**

E

Trees and live without and important other plants that we couldn't
are so useful **them.**

222 THE WORLD

111. Continents and Countries

There are seven large areas of land in the world which we call continents. Asia is the largest of these, followed by Africa, North America, South America, Antarctica, Europe and Australia. There are also far more people living in Asia than any other continent. It has a population of more than 4.5 billion people, six times the number of people living in Europe, and about 60% of the world's population.

Most continents have a number of countries in them. There are 54 countries in Africa, 50 in Europe and 48 countries in Asia. North America has 23 countries, including those in Central America; and South America has 12. The continent of Australia only has one country in it, which is Australia, so it's both a continent and a country, and Antarctica doesn't have any at all. Antarctica is further south than all the other continents and it's also the coldest, the windiest and the least populated continent in the world. Nobody lives there permanently because it's almost completely covered by ice.

*Complete the text by solving the puzzles (A-E) below. The first and last pieces of each puzzle, which are in **bold**, are in the right positions, but the others aren't! Put all the pieces into the correct order and write the words on the dotted lines.*

A

Russia   than   in the   country   other   is larger   any   **world.**

....

....

B

Although   quarters are in   land is   other three   of Europe, the
of Russian   about a quarter   in the continent   **Asia.**

....

....

C

To give country in vast Russia idea of how largest you an part is the is, its European **Europe.**

D

The second of the Ukraine, which a fifth Europe is country in is less than largest **size.**

E

After Russia, Australia and our planet in countries on Brazil, the largest size or surface the US, China, order of their area are Canada, **India.**

224 GRAMMAR PUZZLES

112. Oceans

Salt water covers about 72% of the surface of our planet and almost all of this water is in our seas and five oceans. An ocean is a vast area of water between two continents. They're much larger than seas, and while our seas are partly or completely surrounded by land, our oceans are not. The world's oceans are also extremely deep. Their average depth is almost 3,700 metres. There are many forms of life in our oceans and we depend on the fish and seafood that live in them.

The creatures that live there are amazing, and some of the most wonderful are dolphins and whales. Dolphins are thought to be very intelligent and have been known to protect humans from sharks. Blue whales are bigger and heavier than anything else on our planet. One adult blue whale weighs about the same as 22 African elephants!

*Complete the text by solving the puzzles (A-E) below. The first and last pieces of each puzzle, which are in **bold**, are in the right positions, but the others aren't! Put all the pieces into the correct order and write the words on the dotted lines.*

A

The largest ocean is | east of Asia and South | is west of North | the Pacific, which | America, and **and Australia.**

....

....

B

It is so land in the | world put is greater | than all the **together.** | surface area | large that its

....

....

C

The Ocean which and Europe and the Americas, is the Atlantic is between second largest **Africa.**

D

After the Indian Ocean, order of their and the Arctic other oceans, in Atlantic, the the Southern Ocean size, are the **Ocean.**

E

The Arctic Ocean northern and ocean, it's also the smallest is not only the most **the shallowest.**

113. Languages

English is spoken in more than a hundred countries in the world, more countries than any other language. More people also learn English as a second language than any other language, and it's widely considered to be the international business language. This is because millions of business people use it when they speak or write to native speakers of other languages – that is to say, people whose first language isn't English.

There are, however, two languages which are spoken by more native speakers in the world than English. Almost a billion people are native speakers of Mandarin, the main language in the north and the southwest of China. After Mandarin, more people speak Spanish as a first language than any other. Spanish is spoken by about 400 million people, not only in Spain, but in most of South and Central America, and by Hispanic people in the United States.

*Complete the text by solving the puzzles (A-E) below. The first and last pieces of each puzzle, which are in **bold**, are in the right positions, but the others aren't! Put all the pieces into the correct order and write the words on the dotted lines.*

A

The language English. It's the Australia and New the world is
Canada, Ireland, of native speakers in UK, the US, largest number
main language in the with the third **Zealand.**

....

....

B

After English largest population in language in India, is the most
comes Hindi, which a country with the common first **the world.**

....

....

C

Arabic is the Middle native speakers, Africa and 300 million next, with about are in North most of whom **East.**

D

Portuguese language by spoken as number of is also a large a first **people.**

E

Did you Brazil than in Portuguese in speakers of more native are far know there **Portugal?**

114. World Religions

In the UK and in most countries in the world, people are free to choose their religion. There are four main religions or beliefs in the world: Christianity, Islam, Hinduism and Buddhism. **About a third of all believers are Christians, who believe in God and Jesus Christ. The Christians in Central and South America and Southern Europe are mainly Catholics, and the Christians in North America and Northern Europe are mostly Protestants. The main religion in the Middle East and North Africa is Islam. People who believe in Islam are called Muslims and most are either Sunni or Shia. They believe in Allah, who is their God, and the prophet, Muhammad, who lived more than 1,400 years ago.**

*Complete the text by solving the puzzles (A-E) below. The first and last pieces of each puzzle, which are in **bold**, are in the right positions, but the others aren't! Put all the pieces into the correct order and write the words on the dotted lines.*

A

Hinduism, the | India, and has | practised | religion, is | third largest
many different | mainly in | **Gods.**

....

....

B

Buddhists believe | Asia and South | in God. Most | called | in a teacher
Buddhists live in East | Buddha, but not | **East Asia.**

....

....

C

They practise | and becoming | one thing, | silence by | of other thoughts,
meditation in | clearing the mind | focusing on | **very calm.**

....

....

D

In the | religions, | God | three main | pray to | believers normally **instead.**

....

....

E

There are | called atheists, and | in God, who are | are called | exists, who
know if God | don't believe | also people who | people who don't **agnostics.**

....

....

115. Earth and Other Planets

The world we live in is a planet which is known as Earth. Earth is one of eight planets which orbit a star called the Sun. A group of planets and the star they move around is called a solar system, and ours is one of many solar systems in space. Each planet is the shape of a ball except Saturn, which looks very different from the others. This is because it has rings around it which are made of ice and rock. The planets which are closest to Earth are Venus and Mars, and Earth has its own Moon, which goes round our planet. We see the Moon in the sky at night, and the Sun during the day. The Sun provides energy, and in particular, the heat and light that we need on Earth.

*Complete the text by solving the puzzles (A-E) below. The first and last pieces of each puzzle, which are in **bold**, are in the right positions, but the others aren't! Put all the pieces into the correct order and write the words on the dotted lines.*

A

Life is   have water   Sun would be   planet too   on planets that
only possible   too hot to   close to its   have water. A   **on it.**

B

Any water   a gas. If a   freeze and   water would   from its
and turn into   would boil   Sun, any   far away   planet is too
become ice.

C

Earth is our planet. It's the Sun for life hot and not distance from the right not too to exist on **too cold.**

....

....

D

Although it's some forms of are other planets life on it, we know has systems where the only planet in other solar it's possible there **life also exist.**

....

....

E

Any planet the the right conditions its Sun could have distance from the same Earth and about same size as **for life.**

....

....

GLOBAL PROBLEMS

116. Wars

Wars have been fought throughout history and have had many different causes. Some of the most terrible wars started when one country invaded another country with its army and tried to take control. There have also been civil wars, which happen when two or more groups of people from the same country fight against each other. The two World Wars in the 20th century were fought by a large number of countries. Battles were won and lost. Many different types of weapon were used, most of which were guns or bombs. Soldiers fought on foot and in tanks. Planes attacked each other in the air, and at sea, ships were sunk by submarines.

Innocent civilians became the victims of war.

*Complete the text by solving the puzzles (A-E) below. The first and last pieces of each puzzle, which are in **bold**, are in the right positions, but the others aren't! Put all the pieces into the correct order and write the words on the dotted lines.*

A

| **In the two** | them were | people were | more than a | than half of |
| World Wars, | or died, and more | hundred million | killed, wounded |
| **civilians.** |

....

....

B

Wars between	we can live in	not happen and	century, but
continued in	civil wars have	World War will	countries and
hope that a third	the 21st	there is some	**peace.**

....

....

C

Before could win · believed they · leaders · nuclear · and military weapons, governments **a war.**

....

....

D

With nuclear destroy each · likely to · at war are · countries weapons, **other.**

....

....

E

The dangers these weapons · great that · are so · is not an a war with **option.**

....

....

117. Poverty and Hunger

People who are poor have very little money and few possessions. They live in poverty. In some countries poverty is such a serious problem that people don't have enough food, clean water or clothes. They don't have good enough housing either, and many of them have to live without health care or education. There are about a billion people in the world who live in poverty without the everyday things that most of us have.

Some of the poorest people in the world live in Africa, in countries without enough agriculture or food to provide what people need. A few of these countries are mostly desert, where very little grows, and there isn't enough rain.

*Complete the text by solving the puzzles (A-E) below. The first and last pieces of each puzzle, which are in **bold**, are in the right positions, but the others aren't! Put all the pieces into the correct order and write the words on the dotted lines.*

A

The worst   is called a   rain, which   though, during   weather with no   happen,   disasters   a period of   **drought.**

....

....

B

When   little or   a drought   there's   no water or   there's often   **food.**

....

....

C

People who are very thirsty may drink dirty water which causes disease. Without food or water, they lose weight, become ill and are desperate **for help.**

D

They are so hungry that they starve. International organisations provide aid as soon as they can, but much more could be done to help these people and save their **lives.**

E

There are still millions of men, women and children who try to survive every day without clean water or enough **to eat.**

236 GRAMMAR PUZZLES

118. Disasters

In a famine or a drought, people die because there isn't enough food or water. Other disasters happen when there's too much water. There are floods after days or weeks of heavy rain. Rivers and seas are so full that they flood the land. Houses and roads are under water which causes terrible damage to property. Towns and villages are cut off and have no food or electricity until emergency aid arrives.

Unlike floods, some disasters are unexpected and sudden. Accidents, fires and earthquakes all happen suddenly. An air or road accident, or an accident at sea, can happen in a few seconds. Fires spread so quickly through buildings and dry areas of land that they are soon out of control.

*Complete the text by solving the puzzles (A-E) below. The first and last pieces of each puzzle, which are in **bold**, are in the right positions, but the others aren't! Put all the pieces into the correct order and write the words on the dotted lines.*

A

If there's   injured and   large town,   and people are   a city or a

collapse   earthquake in   a serious   buildings   **killed.**

....

....

B

An   tsunamis. When   produces giant   drown and buildings

coast, people   earthquake under   they reach the   are called

waves which   the sea   **are destroyed.**

....

....

C

There the ocean were were on 2004. Many of the Indian tsunami in holiday next to lived or the people who Ocean in December was a **killed.**

D

After a spread in disaster epidemic. This can serious diseases is sometimes an happen when disaster there **areas.**

E

Thousands of right medical they receive the unless and die become ill people may **help.**

119. Climate Change

Climate change is about changes in the weather that happen over long periods of time. It's caused by natural processes like the heat that comes from the Sun. It's also caused by the movement of rock on the Earth's surface and mountains called volcanos when they erupt. Not all the changes are natural, though. Some human activities have caused changes in our climate and these changes are known as global warming.

Humans and animals breathe out a gas called carbon dioxide and we produce the same gas when we burn fossil fuels. The main fossil fuels are coal, oil and natural gas. We burn these fuels in cars and planes, in factories and in our homes. We burn them to make a huge number of products that we use every day. We also cut down trees and destroy forests all over the world.

*Complete the text by solving the puzzles (A-E) below. The first and last pieces of each puzzle, which are in **bold**, are in the right positions, but the others aren't! Put all the pieces into the correct order and write the words on the dotted lines.*

A

When   dioxide goes   these things,   and causes global   we do all   into the air   carbon   **warming.**

....

....

B

This has   in previous   much   than it did   hundred years   the last   more in   happened   **centuries.**

....

....

C

Our land icebergs are warmer. Our levels are are getting and oceans melting and sea **rising.**

D

There's like droughts and bad weather heatwaves, more very storms.

E

There are global of the changes dying because a serious plants are animals and as well, and more deserts in temperature. It's **problem.**

240 GRAMMAR PUZZLES

120. The Environment

Governments and large companies can do a lot to protect the environment and there are plenty of ways you and I can help as well. When we're at home we could save electricity by switching off most of the lights and other electrical appliances. We'd use less gas if we turned down the central heating or turned off the radiators. Why not have a shower instead of a bath, or use less water when we brush our teeth?

We could try not to throw our rubbish away. Most of it can be recycled. We ought to recycle all our paper and glass. Let's stop buying plastic bags, cups, bottles and cans. If we each had a bag, a cup and a bottle, we'd be able to use them again and again. We could easily read the news online, so we don't need to buy newspapers.

*Complete the text by solving the puzzles (A-E) below. The first and last pieces of each puzzle, which are in **bold**, are in the right positions, but the others aren't! Put all the pieces into the correct order and write the words on the dotted lines.*

A

Food is   and wastes   thousands   pollution   causes   transported   of miles, which   **resources.**

....

....

B

We could   nearby, or   the farm down   produced   food that's   buy   has come from   **the road.**

....

....

GLOBAL PROBLEMS   241

C

Think of all   books and   recycling bank or   go to a   or need. Clothes,
the attic can   no longer use   old things in   some of those   the things
we   **a charity shop.**

D

Why   take public   work every   cars at home and   to drive to
could leave our day when we   do we have   **transport instead?**

E

These are   environment. Let's   put into   wasting things,   ideas we can
protect the   can stop   see how many   and help to   all ways we
action.

THE WEATHER

121. Words for Weather

There are lots of different words in the English language to describe the weather. When we talk about how hot or cold the weather is, it's to do with the temperature. When it's extremely cold we describe the weather as freezing. As the temperature rises above freezing, we might say it's very cold, then cold, then chilly and finally it becomes mild. Mild weather isn't really either hot or cold, but we tend to use the word for a winter's day which doesn't feel cold. At other times of the year when it's colder than we expect it to be, we often say it's not very warm. When temperatures are higher, for example in April or May, we say that it's warm, and in the summer months it can be hot. The temperature in the UK doesn't normally go above 30 degrees Celsius, but when it does some people describe it as boiling or baking.

A number of different words are used to talk about the wind and the rain as well.

*Complete the text by solving the puzzles (A-E) below. The first and last pieces of each puzzle, which are in **bold**, are in the right positions, but the others aren't! Put all the pieces into the correct order and write the words on the dotted lines.*

A

In the   or tornados, but   enough weather   and strong   serious hurricanes   have extreme   UK we don't   we do have gales   to experience   **winds.**

....

....

B

Windy weather   refreshing and   breeze, especially   unpleasant, but   day, can be   is usually   a gentle   on a hot   **pleasant.**

....

....

C

The words we use for rain are to do with how much rain there is. When it's wet or it feels damp. it's stopped, we say it's been raining but

D

Light rain is called drizzle and a short period of rain is frequently a shower.

E

Heavy rain can be described as a downpour, and some of us use the expressions 'it's pouring with rain', and 'it's raining cats and dogs'!

244 GRAMMAR PUZZLES

122. What Weather!

British people love to complain about the weather. A study found that each of us mentions or talks about the weather an average of four times a day! We spend more time talking about the weather than any other subject. We let people know we're unhappy when we think it's too cold, or when the skies are grey and it's cloudy. We do the same when it rains and it's windy, and if it's icy we worry we might slip and fall, so we tell each other to be careful. If we get soaked in the rain or we're freezing cold, that's all we want to talk about. We even complain on the few days every year when it's too hot. At other times, though, we really can be positive about the weather. When there are blue skies and it's warm, we love to talk about it.

*Complete the text by solving the puzzles (A-E) below. The first and last pieces of each puzzle, which are in **bold**, are in the right positions, but the others aren't! Put all the pieces into the correct order and write the words on the dotted lines.*

A

When it's   home, we tell   outside, and   in a warm   how cosy it   room at   cold and raining   each other   we're sitting   **feels.**

....

....

B

We   wait to tell   lightning we can't   exciting, so when   talking about   thunder or see   either. Storms are   unusual weather   can't resist   we hear   **someone.**

....

....

C

Snow's exciting let each heavily, so we snow it's going to too, especially when **other know.**

....

....

D

We love to forecast has weather and tell do that as predict the people what the predicted, so we **well.**

....

....

E

In the first thing much it's often the weather so talking about fact, we enjoy **we mention!**

....

....

246 GRAMMAR PUZZLES

123. The Four Seasons

Spring in the UK is a season with a mixture of different types of weather. In March the weather can be cold and wet and it sometimes snows. April is known for its showers, but it's normally one of the driest months of the year. Most years there isn't much rain in May either, and we notice the days are drier and warmer. During spring (but with climate change in many cases before), flowers appear and birds start building their nests. The days become longer.

Summer is from June until August and is warmer and sunnier than the other seasons. It also has longer days. This is because the UK is in a part of the world that faces the sun in the summer months, so more sunshine and daylight reaches us. In London on the 21st of June, sunrise is at 4.42am and sunset is at 9.20pm. It's usually the longest day of the year with more than sixteen hours of daylight.

Autumn lasts from September to November. It's an unsettled period, which can be cold and wet at times, and there are likely to be more storms than at any other time of year. Flowers die and leaves go brown and fall from the trees.

*Complete the text by solving the puzzles (A-E) below. The first and last pieces of each puzzle, which are in **bold**, are in the right positions, but the others aren't! Put all the pieces into the correct order and write the words on the dotted lines.*

A

Some autumns   mild. This is   October, and   day until   stays warm   the weather   known as an   nights are   even the   during the   **Indian Summer.**

....

....

B

December,   coldest, wettest   February are   months. Winter   and windiest   winter   January and   is the   **season.**

....

....

THE WEATHER 247

C

Towards the becomes even | colder and it end of winter | less wind and rain, but it | there is usually **often snows.**

....

....

D

It also begins 8am and sunset is of December, sunrise | on the 21st days of the **4pm.** | just before is just after | year. In London with the shortest

....

....

E

It's usually the | hours of **daylight.** | day of | about eight | shortest | all with

....

....

248 GRAMMAR PUZZLES

124. Extreme Weather

Of all the continents on Earth, North America, and in particular the United States, has the greatest variety of extremely bad weather conditions, which we often describe as extreme weather. This is mainly due to its location, about halfway between the equator and the North Pole, as well as having the Pacific Ocean to the west and the Atlantic to the east. Cold, dry air from Canada meets the warm tropical air from the oceans and the Gulf of Mexico, which causes the extreme weather. The continent doesn't have a mountain range from west to east that could prevent this from happening.

*Complete the text by solving the puzzles (A-E) below. The first and last pieces of each puzzle, which are in **bold**, are in the right positions, but the others aren't! Put all the pieces into the correct order and write the words on the dotted lines.*

A

As a result, droughts to   has every   weather from   the US   type of   **blizzards.**

....

....

B

It has more   times as many   regions, and ten   tornados a year   and southeastern   than a thousand   mostly in central   on the planet), (or 80% of those   **thunderstorms.**

....

....

C

There are also floods which cause rain and move across year as they hurricanes, torrential throughout the loss of life heatwaves, wildfires, destruction and **the country.**

....

....

D

Europeans experienced compared the weather they of years in the who arrived shocked by to weather in ago were US hundreds **Europe.**

....

....

E

Although weather and Canadians of problem across weather is still forecasts now the dangers, extreme warn Americans a serious **the continent.**

....

....

250 GRAMMAR PUZZLES

125. The Forecast

Good morning. Today in the UK the weather will start very cold and frosty for many of us, with some icy patches, especially in the Southeast. The ice will cause dangerous driving conditions, so if you're driving today, please take care. As the day progresses, it will be mainly dry with some sunny spells, but there will be wintry showers around the coasts, particularly in Wales and Southwest England. Temperatures are unlikely to rise above five degrees Celsius. During the evening, sleet and snow will spread into northwestern areas, where there may well be several centimetres of snow. Elsewhere it will be dry but with the probability of a widespread frost developing. It will be cloudy overnight with some scattered showers.

*Complete the text by solving the puzzles (A-E) below. The first and last pieces of each puzzle, which are in **bold**, are in the right positions, but the others aren't! Put all the pieces into the correct order and write the words on the dotted lines.*

A

Tuesday will   a relatively dry   elsewhere it   showers, mostly   bring more   should be   in the west, but   **day.**

....

....

B

It will   wind, which is   cold in the   on, especially in   feel very   stronger later   likely to get   **the afternoon.**

....

....

C

The outlook of isolated temperatures and Friday is much only a chance Thursday and with rising improved for Wednesday, **showers.**

D

It will feel as high daytime temperatures nights will be although the twelve Celsius, milder, with as eleven or **cold.**

E

It's expected on higher ground in half of the of snow showers rain, but the possibility the north of England week, with less than the first to be drier **and Scotland.**

MONEY AND FINANCE

126. Money and Currencies

Before you visit another country, find out as much as you can about the money used there, and compare how expensive it is to your country. Do some research and check what currency they have and what the exchange rate is. You may not be able to pay for everything with a debit or credit card in the country you're going to, so find out what bank notes and coins they use, what size and shape they are, and how much they're worth. Once you've done this, you'll be able to recognise and count them more easily when you're there, and pay the right amount for anything you buy.

Many European countries have the euro, and if you're travelling from the UK to one of these countries, you'll be asked whether you'd like to pay for something in euros or pounds sterling. And when you arrive in the country you're visiting and use one of the cash machines, you'll be asked whether you want to withdraw money using the local currency or your home currency. It's better to choose the local currency when you pay for something or withdraw money. This is because, by doing so, you'll avoid high exchange rates and the cost of converting your money from pounds to euros.

*Complete the text by solving the puzzles (A-E) below. The first and last pieces of each puzzle, which are in **bold**, are in the right positions, but the others aren't! Put all the pieces into the correct order and write the words on the dotted lines.*

A

While the   a large number   the peso are   Europe, the   also used in

dollar and   currency in   most common   euro is the   **of countries.**

....

....

B

In North   countries as well,   the dollar, and   and Canada have

numerous other   America, the US   including Australia   it's used in

and New Zealand.

....

....

C

In South America, Argentina, Chile, Colombia and Uruguay all have the peso as **their currency.**

D

And in other continents, China has the yuan, Japan has the yen, Russia the rouble and South Africa **the rand.** (9)

E

In total, there are about 180 different currencies in the world, almost as many as there **are countries.**

127. Bank Accounts

Before you choose which bank to join, talk to friends and read as much as you can online. Banks offer different accounts, which pay different amounts of interest, and other benefits that could be useful, like travel and mobile phone insurance. You can open most of them online or by contacting the bank. Some banks and building societies require you to go into your local branch to have a meeting with one of their advisers. They may also ask you to bring an identity card, passport, driving licence or household bill to prove who you are.

*Complete the text by solving the puzzles (A-E) below. The first and last pieces of each puzzle, which are in **bold**, are in the right positions, but the others aren't! Put all the pieces into the correct order and write the words on the dotted lines.*

A

You can likely that account. It's be different you receive will and a savings current account to have a normally choose the interest rates **for each account.**

....

....

B

Interest rates are account and the pounds in your after a year will have a thousand you will earn percentage. If you is 1%, the interest interest rate calculated as a **be ten pounds.**

....

....

MONEY AND FINANCE 255

C

A bank may an overdraft you spend more than you have of a cash machine, allowance. This more money out also give you **in your account.** means they let money, or get

D

This is called being overdrawn money in your you've or in debit. If **are in credit.** got some account you

E

Banks charge if you're overdrawn much higher be careful. Find out when you ask **for an allowance!** being in credit, so interest rates than you receive for what they charge

128. Earning Money

If you get a job in the UK, you'll be given wages or a salary and your employment contract should say how much this is. There is a minimum wage and you can check the exact amount online. You should earn at least this amount per hour, and hopefully more. If you receive a salary, you'll need a bank account so that money can be transferred to your account every month. If you're paid wages, you may receive your payment in cash. Keep any information you get on your monthly or weekly payments. You may need this when you pay tax or complete a tax return at the end of the financial year.

*Complete the text by solving the puzzles (A-E) below. The first and last pieces of each puzzle, which are in **bold**, are in the right positions, but the others aren't! Put all the pieces into the correct order and write the words on the dotted lines.*

A

The financial | in the following | one year and | 5th of April
the UK begins | or tax year in | ends on the | of April in | on the 6th
year.

....

....

B

Inflation is a | expensive because | become more | to the next, so
much the cost | to say how | word we use | in the shops
up from one month | things online and | of living goes | **of inflation.**

....

....

C

In some wages increase they can afford rent, transport and a salary or pay for their jobs people get once a year so to buy food and **other costs.**

....

....

D

If you're a promotion might get job and at your hard, you good you work **at work.**

....

....

E

If you do, earning the salary or an wages so you're get a higher right amount for you should increase in your **your new job.**

....

....

129. Spending Money

It's very easy to spend more money than you earn, which means you'll end up in debt. Owing other people money or being overdrawn at your bank can be a serious financial problem. It's always best to avoid having these problems. A good way of doing this is to have a budget. On the first day of the month, on your laptop or a piece of paper, make a list of all the things you need to pay for or buy during the month. Next to each item, type or write down how much it will cost. When you've finished, compare what you're going to spend with the money you're going to earn and the amount you have in your bank account. Check what you've spent at the end of every week, and make sure you spend less than you earn.

You may be offered a credit card by your bank, which is okay as long as you pay back what you owe every month.

*Complete the text by solving the puzzles (A-E) below. The first and last pieces of each puzzle, which are in **bold**, are in the right positions, but the others aren't! Put all the pieces into the correct order and write the words on the dotted lines.*

A

| **Be careful,** | money to pay | of interest to | have enough | large amount |
| forget, or don't | bill, you'll pay a | though. If you | your credit card |
| **the bank.** |

....

....

B

If you choose a	account, or up	you have in your	able to spend what
allowance agreed	you'll only be	of an overdraft	debit card instead,
to the maximum	**with your bank.**

....

....

C

You may your spending a credit to control card than find it easier with a debit **card.**

....

....

D

Try to stay back what loan to pay bank money, you owe your offered a can. If you in credit if you may be **you owe.**

....

....

E

Like being have to could be though, you'll bank, so it interest to the overdrawn, pay a lot of **expensive.**

....

....

130. Gambling

In the UK, spending money on games of chance is legal, and about a third of the population play the lottery or take part in some form of gambling every month. Some people visit a casino from time to time to play roulette or cards for money, and others go to betting shops. Horse racing used to be the main sport for gambling, but nowadays people can risk their money on almost anything to do with chance. There are so many ways to gamble online that more and more people are winning and losing their money at home. They choose to play online games or to bet on sports which are live. Instead of travelling to a particular sports event, they can watch sport live on their TVs, their computers and phones. It's never been easier to place a bet.

*Complete the text by solving the puzzles (A-E) below. The first and last pieces of each puzzle, which are in **bold**, are in the right positions, but the others aren't! Put all the pieces into the correct order and write the words on the dotted lines.*

A

Gambling a   much larger   serious   spending and losing   be fun, but and again can   money causes   every now   amounts of   few pounds **problems.**

....

....

B

For people who   drugs or   gambling, it's a   control their   addicted to like being   are unable to   type of addiction,   **alcohol.**

....

....

C

The more steal to carry money, they may of their own they run out it back. When become to win desperate they lose, the more money they **on gambling.**

D

Apart addiction can also depression and can cause relationships. It problems, the and destroy from financial result in crime **anxiety.**

E

Help, however, is something about it, a problem and that can help accept they have there are organisations available. When gamblers decide to do **them to stop.**

FOOD AND DRINK

131. Meat

I've eaten meat all my life. In recent years, though, I've become more concerned that animals have to suffer and die for us to eat meat. I've also read that meat can be bad for our health. Eating meat, or at least some meat, is thought to increase the chances of cancer and heart disease. Processed meat, like bacon, sausage and ham, may be worse for us than other meat. Red meat could be less healthy than white meat, and both are less healthy than fish.

I've decided I should probably no longer eat processed or red meat. This would mean no more cooked breakfasts or ham sandwiches for lunch at work. I've always eaten beef, so I would have to give up roast beef, steak, stews and minced meat. The other red meat I've often had is lamb, so I would stop eating roast lamb and chops. Chicken and pork are the only white meats that I've eaten regularly. I've enjoyed duck and turkey as well, but I don't have them very often. I've tended only to eat duck two or three times a year and turkey just once, on Christmas Day!

I never thought I'd give up eating meat altogether, but in the last few months something has changed.

*Complete the text by solving the puzzles (A-E) below. The first and last pieces of each puzzle, which are in **bold**, are in the right positions, but the others aren't! Put all the pieces into the correct order and write the words on the dotted lines.*

A

I've been | more recently | longer contain | foods that no | while now, but | of other | sausages for a | a wide variety | buying vegetarian | I've started eating | **meat.**

....

....

B

I've | become a | could, and | time in my | realised for | probably should, | life that I | the first | **vegetarian.**

....

....

C

I'm concerned about animal welfare and, as I get older, I'm more concerned about my own health, and what's **good for me.**

D

Vegetarian and vegan food is now widely available in supermarkets and shops, and it tastes so much better than it used to years **ago.**

E

There are plenty of reasons why it makes sense to stop eating meat, and it's never been easier to **do.**

132. Fish and Seafood

Some of the best fresh fish in the UK are served in fish and chip shops and restaurants on the coast. The fishing boats arrive with their catch early in the morning, and by lunchtime the same day, the fish appear in local towns, on menus and plates, or in paper or plastic bags to take away. In fish and chip shops there's often a choice of cod, haddock or plaice, fried in batter (which is a mixture of eggs, milk and flour), but a much wider variety of fresh fish is available elsewhere. Turbot, sea bass, sole and halibut, for example, are served in fish and seafood restaurants, and there's a great deal of fresh fish to choose from in fishmongers' shops and some supermarkets. Tinned fish, though, is sold in supermarkets in large quantities, and tinned tuna, salmon, and sardines can be found in almost any shop selling food in tins. Most of us prefer fish that's freshly cooked, but there are good reasons to buy tinned fish as well. It can be kept at home as long as you want, it's rich in healthy oils, and it's relatively cheap.

Other fish can be bought frozen in shops and supermarkets. A popular frozen food, especially for children, is fish fingers, which are smaller pieces of fish covered in breadcrumbs. Fishcakes, which are round pieces of fish mixed with potato, are also covered in breadcrumbs and can be bought either fresh or frozen. Another frozen food that people buy and is covered in either breadcrumbs or batter, is scampi, or Dublin Bay prawns.

*Complete the text by solving the puzzles (A-E) below. The first and last pieces of each puzzle, which are in **bold**, are in the right positions, but the others aren't! Put all the pieces into the correct order and write the words on the dotted lines.*

A

Eating   enjoy   ways to   of many   prawns   is only one   as scampi   **prawns, though.**

....

....

B

They're   shrimps - mainly   popular seafood in   they're called   because they're   the most   the US - where   both the UK and   **so versatile.**

....

....

C

Prawns are numerous other with avocado, and soups and curries, garlic, with delicious in noodles, in salads, spaghetti, rice or **foods.**

D

Other restaurants across crab, scallops, include fresh served in seafood options which are mussels and oysters, **the world.**

E

We only eat less expensive time to prepare occasions because they're much expensive, but home on special and can be they take them at **than lobster!**

133. Vegetables

Vegetables are very good for us. They're full of vitamins and protect us from serious diseases, so they're an important part of a healthy diet. We don't usually eat one vegetable on its own, though, because most of us enjoy them much more when we have them with other vegetables or food. Salads are a good example. Lettuce doesn't taste of much without anything else, but adding other vegetables makes a big difference. Try it with chopped onions and peppers, some small tomatoes, cucumber and a salad dressing. You'll probably enjoy it more.

*Complete the text by solving the puzzles (A-E) below. The first and last pieces of each puzzle, which are in **bold**, are in the right positions, but the others aren't! Put all the pieces into the correct order and write the words on the dotted lines.*

A

Vegetables go with new foods too. Have and sprouts, or fish chicken with carrots potatoes and you tried well with other **peas?**

....

....

B

Another dish and cauliflower and steak in a peppercorn recommend is and spinach, dish called cauliflower such a good sauce with mushrooms I would combination there's a cheese are **cheese!**

....

....

C

What about cold as well, especially any cooked dish broccoli? They're tasty in salads on they're enjoyable green beans and served hot, but as part of almost **a warm day.**

D

In the larder to make vegetables in not use the cold, why a hot vegetable when it's winter, though, your fridge or **soup?**

E

There are ask a ways of vegetables. Just different eating hundreds of **vegetarian!**

134. Fruit

Preparing a fruit salad for a large family doesn't take long. First of all, choose your favourite fruit and buy it from your local market, greengrocer's or supermarket. Wash all the fruit in cold water before you start to prepare it.

This is a recipe I made up recently for my family, but you can put any fruit you like in a fruit salad.

Take a pineapple and cut off the top and the bottom of the fruit. Carefully remove the thick skin before cutting it into smaller chunks. (Chunks are thick pieces of food.) Peel seven oranges, divide two of them into segments (the small parts of a piece of fruit), and cut the segments in half. When you've done this, take the skin off two apples and a melon, and cut them into smaller chunks, but make sure you take out the middle parts and the pips. Now slice two peaches into smaller pieces and remove the stones from the middle of the fruit, before cutting some cherries in half and taking their stones out as well.

*Complete the text by solving the puzzles (A-E) below. The first and last pieces of each puzzle, which are in **bold**, are in the right positions, but the others aren't! Put all the pieces into the correct order and write the words on the dotted lines.*

A

The next   three   is to slice   and strawberries   thing to do   into two or   some grapes   **pieces.**

....

....

B

To make   fruit in as   water, before   add about the   that are left into   the five oranges   the juice, squeeze   putting all the   same amount of   a large bowl and   **well.**

....

....

C

Raspberries, pears, and fruit you might include. Be kiwifruit are want to careful with **bananas, though.** three other

D

They lose their colour and juice for too long, so put them mushy if they're left in the in at the last **minute!** go brown and

E

Finally, when add some yoghurt, and put your fruit salad, why not a spoonful of you serve **top?** honey on

135. Drinks

There are plenty of soft drinks in shops and supermarkets and many of them are bad for us. Some fizzy drinks and energy drinks have a lot of sugar in them. It's a good idea to check how much sugar there is by reading the label. If you buy fizzy drinks, it's best to choose diet ones. There's also sugar in drinks like orange squash and orange juice. At home and at school, most children drink milk. Adults drink a lot of coffee and tea at home and at work. At night before they go to bed, some people have warm milk, hot chocolate or herbal teas. Camomile and other herbal teas help us relax and have a good night's sleep.

Alcoholic drinks are available almost everywhere. Pubs and bars sell different types of beer. In the UK customers can order a pint or half a pint of lager or bitter.

*Complete the text by solving the puzzles (A-E) below. The first and last pieces of each puzzle, which are in **bold**, are in the right positions, but the others aren't! Put all the pieces into the correct order and write the words on the dotted lines.*

A

| **There's sweet** | rum and | of white, red | too, like whisky, | and a choice |
| are spirits | or dry cider | wines. There | or rosé | **vodka.** |

....

....

B

| **Spirits are very** | too much of | content, so it's | have high |
| dangerous to drink | because they | strong, though, | alcoholic | **them.** |

....

....

C

Choose a drinks like of spirits are normally instead. Cocktails and soft a mixture cocktail **fruit juice.**

D

Better still, restaurants you sparkling water In most drink water! in bottles, or tap can ask bars and for still or **water.**

E

To stay much as two drink at least day. Women are need to drink half litres a healthy we day, and men as water every one and a advised to **litres.**

272 COOKING AND RESTAURANTS

136. Breakfast and Brunch

In the UK, we usually have breakfast quite soon after we get up. As we get up at different times, breakfast can be any time from about 6am to 10am. Some people have cereal or porridge. If they're hungry, they might also have bread or toast with butter and marmalade, or jam. Others have a cooked breakfast, which may include a selection of bacon, vegetarian, vegan or pork sausages, eggs, tomatoes, mushrooms and baked beans. The eggs are usually fried, scrambled or poached, but boiled eggs can be eaten on their own or with a piece of toast and butter.

*Complete the text by solving the puzzles (A-E) below. The first and last pieces of each puzzle, which are in **bold**, are in the right positions, but the others aren't! Put all the pieces into the correct order and write the words on the dotted lines.*

A

Hot orange breakfast, coffee are drinks, like and cold as tea and drinks such drunk at **juice, are too.**

....

....

B

There's a brunch. The word breakfast and lunch and the last four 'brunch' is a combination meal between letters of 'breakfast' of the first two which is called **letters of 'lunch'.**

....

....

C

Not everyone had a late breakfast, so it's people have brunch up too late for eats brunch. Some perfect if you've when they get **night.**

D

The food more like similar can be different, often or very to breakfast, **lunch.**

E

Ham, served as brunch, food is available in fruit and bread for breakfast or eggs, yoghurt, cheese, boiled and this type of most hotels either are frequently **brunch.**

137. Lunch, Tea, and Supper

Most of us have breakfast in the morning, lunch in the middle of the day, and supper, or dinner, in the evening. When we go out to a restaurant in the evening, the meal is normally called dinner, especially on more formal occasions. Supper is an informal evening meal at home, so most of us have supper much more often than dinner. For formal lunch and dinner there may be three courses: a starter, a main course and a dessert. There's often a choice, too, between a dessert and cheese. At work, though, most people have less time for a meal and may only have a short break to eat a sandwich before they carry on working.

*Complete the text by solving the puzzles (A-E) below. The first and last pieces of each puzzle, which are in **bold**, are in the right positions, but the others aren't! Put all the pieces into the correct order and write the words on the dotted lines.*

A

This takes a lot | home, which | Sunday lunch at | a restaurant, or | from lunch in | is very different | **longer.**

....

....

B

Tea is usually afternoon, | a tearoom, hotel | which people | home, or in | either at | have in the | a light meal | **or restaurant.**

....

....

C

It might just be a pot or a cup of tea, but biscuits, scones, cake, and even sandwiches, are often part of afternoon **tea as well.**

D

The words used for meals, though, can be confusing. Different words are used in the north of England and other parts **of the country.**

E

For example, tea in many family homes in the UK is an early supper, especially for children, rather than a cup of tea in **the afternoon.**

138. Cooking at Home

This is my recipe for spaghetti Bolognese. Start by taking a large onion. Peel, slice, and then chop it into small pieces. I always wear swimming goggles when I do this, so the onions don't sting my eyes and make me cry. Heat a couple of tablespoons of olive oil in a large saucepan, add the onions and fry them gently. While this is happening, take some garlic, remove the skin, and put it through a garlic crusher. When the onions have gone brown, add some minced beef, which we call mince, and fry it for about a minute next to the onions. Pour half a litre of water into the saucepan, mix it with the mince and the onions until it boils, and leave it all to simmer on a low heat. Put the garlic and some tinned tomatoes in the saucepan.

*Complete the text by solving the puzzles (A-E) below. The first and last pieces of each puzzle, which are in **bold**, are in the right positions, but the others aren't! Put all the pieces into the correct order and write the words on the dotted lines.*

A

Add a   wine and three   bay leaves   cube, a   beef stock   of red glass   or four   **to the mixture.**

....

....

B

Stir the contents   spoon every ten   at least an   low heat for with a wooden   the sauce on a   carefully   minutes and cook of the saucepan   **hour.**

....

....

COOKING AND RESTAURANTS 277

C

Now take a small pieces with some parsley into cheese and
put it in another scissors and a small bowl. Cut Parmesan a pair of
grate it into chunk of **bowl.**

D

Boil water for about saucepan. Take the it in the boiling
into a separate the packet and cook pour the water spaghetti from
a kettle and **ten minutes.**

E

When from the water and parsley soft, separate it the cheese
the spaghetti is and sprinkle and the sauce serve the spaghetti
with a sieve. Now **on top.**

139. Eating in Restaurants

When you go into a restaurant, there's normally a waiter to greet you. If it's a popular restaurant it's always best to book a table in advance. The waiter might ask you whether you've booked and then take you to your table, or try to find you one. Once you've sat down, you'll be able to look at the menu and order some drinks. In some restaurants there are tablecloths and napkins on the tables and there's normally cutlery for every customer. There may also be salt, pepper and slices of bread. Read the menu carefully and decide how many courses you would like. If you're hungry you could have a starter, a main course and a dessert or cheese at the end of the meal.

*Complete the text by solving the puzzles (A-E) below. The first and last pieces of each puzzle, which are in **bold**, are in the right positions, but the others aren't! Put all the pieces into the correct order and write the words on the dotted lines.*

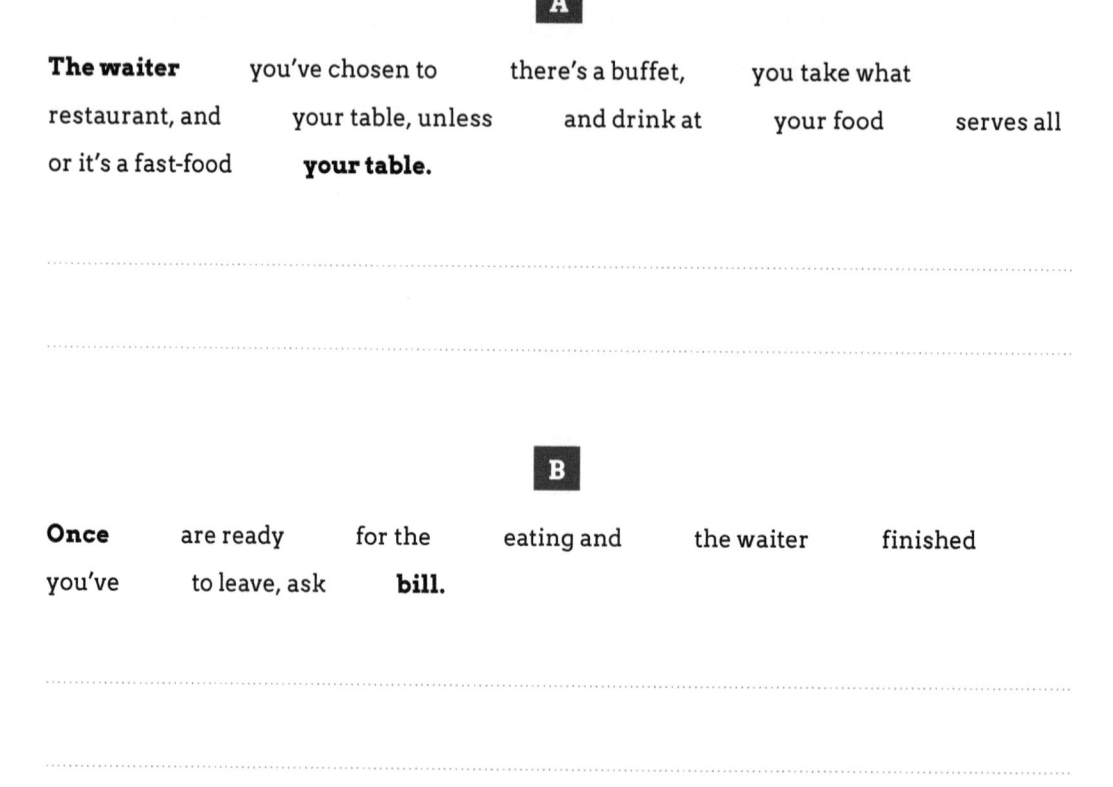

A

The waiter | you've chosen to | there's a buffet, | you take what
restaurant, and | your table, unless | and drink at | your food | serves all
or it's a fast-food | **your table.**

B

Once | are ready | for the | eating and | the waiter | finished
you've | to leave, ask | **bill.**

C

When it's to your *(how you want)* *(brought)* *(tell the waiter)* *(need to)* *(table you'll)* **to pay.**

D

If you're debit *(the waiter will)* *(paying by)* *(or credit card)* *(use a card)* *(you can make)* **your payment.** *(machine so)*

E

Service included, but *(if it's not, you)* *(may wish)* *(a tip for)* **serving you.** *(is usually)* *(the waiter)* *(to give)*

280 GRAMMAR PUZZLES

140. Food from Other Countries

In London and other capital cities, you can try food from a lot of different countries in the world. The UK is famous for its fish and chips, and it's also known for roast beef and Yorkshire pudding. But it's the food from other countries that gives people so much choice. Couscous is a North African food from countries like Algeria and Morocco, which is normally eaten with meat or vegetables. Moules frites – French for mussels and chips – is a Belgian dish which is also common in France. Crepes, or pancakes, are popular in France too, and even snails and frogs' legs are eaten there!

*Complete the text by solving the puzzles (A-E) below. The first and last pieces of each puzzle, which are in **bold**, are in the right positions, but the others aren't! Put all the pieces into the correct order and write the words on the dotted lines.*

A

The Germans have   Frankfurt - and hamburgers   frankfurters were   their sausages - their   were named   the city of   brought us   named after **after Hamburg.**

....

....

B

Pastries, which   shops, are   they were originally   pastries because   and coffee   in most bakers'   can be bought   called Danish **from Denmark.**

....

....

C

Greek restaurants | all over the | are famous | Indian ones offer
like moussaka, | world for their | serve specialities | the Italians
with rice, and | curry dishes | **pizza and pasta.**

....

....

D

If you go | Japanese | dishes, and if | restaurant you can | fish you'll enjoy
their tapas | you like raw | to a Spanish | eat some of | **sushi.**

....

....

E

There are | time in a city | world to list them | as many of them
from around the | Paris, why not try | you spend | too many foods
like London or | all here, but if | **as you can?**

....

....

SHOPPING AND SHOPS

141. The History of Shopping

Shopping has been a human activity for thousands of years. In ancient Greece and Rome there were places called markets where people could buy things. There were stalls in the markets where everything on sale was displayed so customers could examine the goods and decide what they wanted. Even then, people had a good idea of what they were going to buy before they arrived at the market. We know this because the earliest known shopping list in the UK was written about two thousand years ago by a Roman soldier. It was discovered near Hadrian's Wall, which is in Northumberland, a county in the north of England.

*Complete the text by solving the puzzles (A-E) below. The first and last pieces of each puzzle, which are in **bold**, are in the right positions, but the others aren't! Put all the pieces into the correct order and write the words on the dotted lines.*

A

The   goods were   18th   which   with windows   the late   first shops   in London in   displayed   **century.**

....

....

B

Shop owners   sell in their   arranged everything   they used   needed to   realised they   they wanted to   advertisements and   attract customers, so   **shop windows.**

....

....

C

In the items in a wide stores were the first department range of opened with 19th century **different departments.**

D

Later in the same shop to another walk from one customers could built indoors so centres were on, shopping **building.**

E

Some shopping found outside can be towns, but others centres are in cities and **urban areas.**

142. Shops

Department stores and supermarkets in the UK sell a large number of different goods, and almost anything can be bought online. Many of the shops in shopping centres and the high street, however, specialise in one type of product. There are clothes shops, sports shops and toy shops, bakers' that sell bread, and coffee shops that can make you a coffee. Jewellers' display jewellery like rings and watches, and florists' sell flowers. Pet shops have plenty of things for dogs, cats and rabbits. If you're looking for something for your home or garden, go to your furniture shop, hardware store, or gardening centre, and for something old and interesting, try the antique shop. Stationery shops are useful for work, school and free time, and electrical shops can help you with all those appliances in the flat.

In recent decades, computer stores, phone shops and fast-food places have appeared on our streets. Fast-food restaurants sell hamburgers, chicken, or sandwiches, and some offer healthy food too. Why not buy your meat at the local butcher's, though, or your vegetables at the greengrocer's?

*Complete the text by solving the puzzles (A-E) below. The first and last pieces of each puzzle, which are in **bold**, are in the right positions, but the others aren't! Put all the pieces into the correct order and write the words on the dotted lines.*

A

You can get   agents on the   bathroom from your   anything you want
find a   help you   high street will   the estate   local chemist's, and
to keep in your   your medicines or   **property.**

B

If you   store on the   is the place   your street   items, the convenience
two everyday   need just one or   corner of   **to go.**

C

There but not a shop everything, to be for almost used **anymore.**

....

....

D

Online home have need to your way shopping is anything you that deliver and companies changed the shopping **done.**

....

....

E

Shops are make any they can't day, especially every streets, because in our high closing down **money.**

....

....

143. Clothes Shopping

When I went into the clothes shop, all the shop assistants were busy helping other customers. This gave me time to look at the clothes that were on sale and see if there was anything that I liked enough to buy. There was a shirt and a pair of trousers that I liked, but they were the wrong size. A shop assistant finished serving another customer and walked over to me. She smiled and asked me whether she could help. I showed her the clothes I had found and explained that I needed a different size. She said she would check whether they had my size in stock in the storeroom. As soon as she had gone, another assistant offered to help me. I thanked her, but said that I was already being served. The first assistant then came back carrying a shirt on a hanger. She said the trousers were out of stock but she had found a shirt that was my size. I told her I'd like to try it on, so she took me to the changing rooms.

*Complete the text by solving the puzzles (A-E) below. The first and last pieces of each puzzle, which are in **bold**, are in the right positions, but the others aren't! Put all the pieces into the correct order and write the words on the dotted lines.*

A

| **The shirt** | suited me as | the mirror | whether it | looked in |
| perfectly. I | fitted me | to check | **well.** | |

....

....

B

| **I thought** | to buy it, took | put my own | so I decided | good on me |
| it off, and | it looked | **one back on.** | | |

....

....

C

When I the assistant room I told shirt I'd just take the the changing came out of that I would **tried on.**

D

We put it in a the shirt and plastic where she took the cash desk went over to **bag.**

E

She asked I did. Then I help, and left in my size, so her for her some trousers new shirt, thanked like to order me if I would paid for my **the shop.**

144. Supermarkets

Before you go to the supermarket, it's a good idea to check what you need and write a shopping list. If there isn't a supermarket near where you live, you'll need to go to one by car or public transport. Large supermarkets normally have car parks which customers can use, and unlike other car parks, are free. When you arrive at the entrance of the supermarket, get a trolley if you're going to do a lot of shopping, or a basket if you only need a few things. You can attach your shopping list to the front of some trolleys, which makes shopping easier. If you know where everything is, you'll find what you're looking for quickly.

Fruit and vegetables are usually in the same area, and meat and fish are nearby. Dairy products like milk and yoghurt are all together, and so are most tinned soups, meat, fish and vegetables.

*Complete the text by solving the puzzles (A-E) below. The first and last pieces of each puzzle, which are in **bold**, are in the right positions, but the others aren't! Put all the pieces into the correct order and write the words on the dotted lines.*

A

Pasta, cereals,	one or two of	packets, and much	on shelves in
likely to be	are mostly in	of this food is	biscuits and tea	**the aisles.**

....

....

B

Drinks are all	beer, wine	and cans of soft	ones, like	well, with bottles
alcoholic	location as	drinks near	in the same	

and spirits.

....

....

SHOPPING AND SHOPS 289

C

You can you need for you'll find there's something or your bathroom, a supermarket. If anything in cat, your kitchen buy almost your family, dog or **it there.**

D

There's always meat, fish, and freezers are well. Supermarket of frozen food as frozen vegetables, food, but plenty a lot of fresh usually full of **ice cream.**

E

Make sure, when you get to pay. If you before you go still be frozen trolley just put it in your though, you do, it should **home!**

145. Shopping Online

Shopping online gives us more information about different products than we've ever had before. If you're looking for something online, use a search engine to find the companies that sell it. Price comparison sites compare how much different companies are charging for the same product. Do some research on these sites and you're likely to pay less than if you just walked into a shop and bought the product. Online shopping's convenient too. You can shop anywhere and at any time, day or night.

Although it helps if someone you know recommends a product, it's important to read the reviews written by customers about a company before you decide whether to buy or pay for something. By doing this, you often learn a lot more about the quality of a product or a service, and the number of stars given by customers can also be helpful. I recently found a company that had excellent reviews and provided me with a very good product and service. Their website had all the information I needed, and I was able to search for and find exactly what I wanted. I entered my personal details online, made the payment and purchased the product. They sent several texts to inform me where the product was and when it would be delivered. It arrived at my home address in less than 24 hours.

*Complete the text by solving the puzzles (A-E) below. The first and last pieces of each puzzle, which are in **bold**, are in the right positions, but the others aren't! Put all the pieces into the correct order and write the words on the dotted lines.*

A

Customers,   when they   different   have a very   shop   though, can   experience   **online.**

B

If you read   reviews warn you   what you'll   company and the   that's probably   terrible products,   service or   about a   about awful   **get.**

C

They may don't waste companies with a product, but or money on to buy if you want you quickly any time get back to **bad reviews.**

....

....

D

Many of them contact them about you try to to reach when a product you've if not impossible are very difficult, a problem with **already bought.**

....

....

E

If you're send them an reading their a company after them, to see how text, or call email or a reviews, why not still unsure about **they respond?**

....

....

PEOPLE

146. What Women Wear

In the morning when we get up, we get dressed, or put on our clothes. During the day we wear our clothes. Before we go to bed at night, we get undressed, or take off our clothes.

Women wear underwear, which is normally a bra and knickers. Over their underwear, some women wear jeans, trousers or shorts, with a shirt or T-shirt. Others wear dresses, or a blouse and a skirt. Businesswomen and women at work tend to wear formal clothes, such as a suit, which is a jacket with matching trousers or a matching skirt. Women also wear stockings or tights, but when it's cold, or to go running or play sports, many prefer leggings.

*Complete the text by solving the puzzles (A-E) below. The first and last pieces of each puzzle, which are in **bold**, are in the right positions, but the others aren't! Put all the pieces into the correct order and write the words on the dotted lines.*

A

In winter, they | on their hands to | they go out. On | sweater, and put
boots, and gloves | and a scarf when | may also wear a | wear shoes or
on a coat, a hat | their feet they | **keep them warm.**

....

....

B

More women | bracelets on their | fingers, and | wear necklaces
jewellery. They | on their | and earrings, rings | than men wear | **wrists.**

....

....

C

Women also we use the used for wearing wear make-up, and verbs that are it's worn as the same verbs to describe how **clothes.**

D

Women put the morning, wear it during the day or in and then take make-up on in the evening **it off.**

E

There are many different make-up, but two of the types of **and mascara.** are lipstick most popular

147. What Men Wear

In the morning, when we get up, we get dressed, or put on our clothes. During the day we wear our clothes. Before we go to bed at night, we get undressed, or take off our clothes.

The general word for underwear that most men wear is pants (the long word is underpants), and there's a choice of boxer shorts, trunks, or briefs. When it's cold, some men wear a vest.

*Complete the text by solving the puzzles (A-E) below. The first and last pieces of each puzzle, which are in **bold**, are in the right positions, but the others aren't! Put all the pieces into the correct order and write the words on the dotted lines.*

A

Over these clothes   sports, a lot of   trousers below it,   they're playing   the waist, and   hot, or when   a shirt above   they usually wear   but when it's   **men wear shorts.**

....

....

B

Businessmen   their shirt   tie, but nowadays   top button of   are at work prefer   shirt and a   to undo the   most men who   wear a formal   used to   **instead.**

....

....

C

Many of them and matching the shirt, or is a jacket a suit, which jacket over wear a **trousers.**

D

When casual clothes, home they jeans, a T-shirt men wear men are at of young and a lot wear more **and trainers.**

E

Older men usually shoes have laces black or brown, and shoes on their any colour. Some wear socks but they can be feet. Most shoes are **and others don't.**

148. The Body

For students learning English, it's useful to learn the words used for different parts of the body. One way of doing this is to describe which parts are next to each other. Every human body has a head (at the top), which contains a brain, which we use to think. At the top of the head we have hair (except bald men and some babies). Our ears are on each side of the head, and at the front there's a face with two eyes, a nose and a mouth. Below the mouth is a chin, and below the chin is a neck, which connects the head to the rest of the body. The front of the neck is called the throat. Below the neck is a chest, at the front, and a back, at the back! Human beings have shoulders on each side which are at the top of our arms. We bend our arms at the elbows, and at the end of our arms there are hands. On each hand we have four fingers and a thumb.

*Complete the text by solving the puzzles (A-E) below. The first and last pieces of each puzzle, which are in **bold**, are in the right positions, but the others aren't! Put all the pieces into the correct order and write the words on the dotted lines.*

A

Below stomach, is above is the the chest which **the waist.**

....

....

B

Below the waist which is our hips, the bottom, side are just above on each which are **below the back.**

....

....

C

Below bend at which two legs, we have the bottom **our knees.**

D

At the between each leg the body called feet, and in there's a part of legs are two and each foot end of the **the ankle.**

E

Each foot ends our head to toes. This from has five journey **toe!**

298 GRAMMAR PUZZLES

149. The Family

The day my sister got married, the weather couldn't have been better. The sun was shining and the skies above were bright blue. The wedding ceremony was in a beautiful, old church in the village.

At the end of the service, we walked slowly out of the church. The photographer approached us and asked us all to pose for photos with the bride and groom. I've still got some of the photos and they remind me how special the occasion was. There's one in particular I like. Almost everyone in the family is in the picture. My sister and her husband are in the front row, in the middle.

*Complete the text by solving the puzzles (A-E) below. The first and last pieces of each puzzle, which are in **bold**, are in the right positions, but the others aren't! Put all the pieces into the correct order and write the words on the dotted lines.*

A

My mother	and grandfather),	them, and my mother's	front, next to
standing beside	and father are	are also at the	parents (my grandmother
my father.			

....

....

B

| **My aunt, uncle,** | background, in | my nephew | all in the | and niece, are |
| older brother, and | **the row behind.** | | | |

....

....

C

My age as just in front the same standing cousin, who's
I am, is **of my uncle.**

D

All the members on the day of newly-wed couple. I know are on the
now, but I didn't who they are other side of the of the groom's family
the wedding.

E

I'd met my time I met other on several occasions, family was at
brother-in-law members of his but the first **the reception.**

150. Life and Death

There's a saying that only two things are certain in life: death and taxes. It was said by Benjamin Franklin in the 18th century and it could be true today. We still pay taxes and we're not here forever. Let's make the most of every day, be kind to other people, and work hard at everything we do.

There's also a prayer that says we should accept the things we can't change and have the wisdom to change the things we can. Death is the normal and natural end of life. There's nothing we can do about it. We can, however, change the lives of elderly people and the experience of those at the end of their lives. In recent decades there have been global reports on the quality of life for people over the age of sixty. The reports have concluded that the elderly in countries like Switzerland, Norway and Sweden, have better health, pensions, employment and care than anywhere else. The rest of the world can learn from these countries.

*Complete the text by solving the puzzles (A-E) below. The first and last pieces of each puzzle, which are in **bold**, are in the right positions, but the others aren't! Put all the pieces into the correct order and write the words on the dotted lines.*

A

Governments have   care, especially when   people in need   to make sure   or frail in old   receive proper   a responsibility   they become ill   **age.**

....

....

B

People who are   treatment and drugs   in history, so their   painful and   given better medical   pain can now be   suffering or in   than at any time   experience is less   **difficult.**

....

....

C

With advances in medical science, a priority possible for those who are near **life.** be to make this century should the end of dying as painless as

D

When someone dies, we should after the peace, before, they are at **funeral.** remember during, and

E

Finally, if ashes into throw their it's their a place they **once loved.** the wind, in wish, let's

SOLUTIONS

Adults *(Topic 59)*
A. Adults / choose / how / to spend / their / money and / where to / save it. (8)
B. They follow / a religion, a political / party, or a sports / team. They make / decisions about / the sports they / play and their / pastimes. (8)
C. What type / of music or / radio programme / should they listen / to? Do they decide / to spend / time reading, and / if so, what do / they read? (9)
D. What TV / channels, films, or / plays should / they watch? They / choose the social / media they're / interested / in, and who and / when to call, email / or text. (10)
E. It can't / be easy / being an adult / in the modern / world. They must be / very grown-up / to make / so many / decisions! (9)

Airports *(Topic 87)*
A. Once you've / arrived / at the airport / and found the / right terminal, / check the / screens which give / you information / about your flight. (9)
B. They tell / you if your / flight is on / time or / delayed. They / also tell you / which gate / to go to when / it's time to / board your / plane. (11)
C. It's a good idea / to check / in as soon / as you arrive. When / you check in, you / show your ticket / and give your / bags to the person / who's working / for the airline / you're flying with. (11)
D. You're allowed / to take hand / luggage with you / and put it in / the lockers above / your seat, but not / larger cases and / bags. These are placed / in the hold. (9)
E. As soon as / you've checked in / you can / go to the / departure / lounge. Have / a good / flight! (8)

Alexander Fleming *(Topic 5)*
A. If it could / kill bacteria / in a dish, / Fleming realised / it might be / able to kill / bacteria that / cause disease / in humans and / animals. (10)
B. He managed / to grow the mould / on its own / and discovered / it produced a / substance that / destroyed a range of / different bacteria. (8)
C. He called / the substance / penicillin, but didn't / think it could be / produced in large / enough quantities, or last / long enough in the / human body, to / treat infection. (9)
D. In the / 1940s, however, / other scientists / showed this could / be done, and penicillin / was one of a number / of antibiotics / that changed / the world of medicine / forever. (10)
E. The substance / discovered / by Fleming / became a / drug that / saves millions / of lives / every year. (8)

American Politics *(Topic 24)*
A. California has / the largest / population, so it / also has the / largest number of / representatives, which / can be more / than fifty. States with / the smallest populations / have only one / representative. (11)
B. In total, there / are 100 senators / and 435 representatives / in Congress, who / are either Democrat / or Republican / politicians. (7)

C. Democrats, / who tend / to be more / left-wing, normally / support higher / taxes, and more / money for public / services such / as health / care and education. (10)
D. Republicans tend / to be more / right-wing and / believe in the / right to possess / guns, and / the death / penalty. (8)
E. Their / policies usually / result in lower / taxes, but less / money for public / services and / increased military / spending. (8)

An Evening In *(Topic 80)*
A. When my / flatmates get / home we / decide what we're / going / to do and quite / often we choose / what we're going / to watch on / TV. (10)
B. We sometimes / watch a / film, often an / action movie / or a comedy, but / we also like / documentaries, news / and sports / programmes. (9)
C. At the / end of the / news we watch / the weather / forecast so we / know what the / weather's going / to be like / the next day. (9)
D. We normally cook / something at / home, but at / the weekend we / sometimes order / a home / delivery / pizza or an Indian / curry. (9)
E. We could / get a take / away or go / out to eat / because there's / a restaurant near / where we / live, but in / winter, once we get / home, we usually / prefer to stay in. (11)

Bank Accounts *(Topic 127)*
A. You can / normally choose / to have a / current account / and a savings / account. It's / likely that / the interest rates / you receive will / be different / for each account. (11)
B. Interest rates are / calculated as a / percentage. If you / have a thousand / pounds in your / account and the / interest rate / is 1%, the interest / you will earn / after a year will / be ten pounds. (11)

C. A bank may / also give you / an overdraft / allowance. This / means they let / you spend more / money, or get / more money out / of a cash machine, / than you have / in your account. (11)
D. This is called / being overdrawn / or in debit. If / you've / got some / money in your / account you / are in credit. (8)
E. Banks charge / much higher / interest rates / if you're overdrawn / than you receive for / being in credit, so / be careful. Find out / what they charge / when you ask / for an allowance! (10)

Barbara Jordan *(Topic 19)*
A. Barbara / Jordan was / a lawyer, Democratic / politician, and a / leader of / the civil / rights / movement. (8)
B. In 1966 she / became the first / black woman / to win a seat / in the Texas / Senate, and the / first African American / member of the / Senate since / 1883. (10)
C. In 1972 she was / elected to / Congress, the first / woman to represent / Texas in the / House of / Representatives in her / own right. (8)
D. She / is best / known, / though, for / two important / political / speeches. (7)
E. In 1974 she / made a / televised / speech / supporting / the impeachment / of the American / president, Richard / Nixon. (9)

Bathroom Things *(Topic 74)*
A. On the / bottom shelf / there's a bottle / of aftershave, for / me, and a / bottle of scent, / which is sometimes / called perfume, / that my wife / uses. (10)
B. I keep /other things / on the bottom / shelf as / well, including a / deodorant, which / I use under / my arms, a hairbrush / so I can brush / my hair, and a / comb if I want / to comb it. (12)
C. Below the / basin there's / a cupboard / where we / keep toilet / rolls, bottles / of shampoo, and / shower / gel. (9)

D. We keep / packets of / soap and toothpaste / there as / well, in / case we run / out of / anything. (8)
E. This is / also where / I put my / washbag which / I put everything / in whenever / we go / away. (8)

Biology *(Topic 46)*
A. Biology is also / about nutrition, / digestion and / excretion, or in / other words, what / goes into the / body, how it's / broken down / inside, and then / how it leaves / the body. (11)
B. It's / about respiration and / breathing, too, and / how gases such / as oxygen, / carbon dioxide / and hydrogen, are / essential to life. (8)
C. In animals, / blood / transports / everything / needed / around / a circulation / system. (8)
D. In plants, / water / is moved from / the roots to the / leaves, and food is / carried from / the leaves to the / rest of the plant. (8)
E. Whatever's / required, / nature finds / a way of / providing / it, and biology / is a way of / learning / about it. (9)

Birds *(Topic 108)*
A. People / put bird / tables in their / gardens so they / can watch / birds from / their kitchen / windows. (8)
B. They / give / them / food and / water, especially / in the / winter. (7)
C. Birdwatching / is a popular / hobby. We love / to watch birds / because they're / beautiful and amazing / creatures, but / they need to / be protected. (9)
D. There are / at least 10,000 / species of / birds in the / world, and / there may be as / many as 18,000 / according / to some reports. (9)
E. A large / number of / these species, / however, probably / well over / a thousand, are in / danger of / extinction. (8)

Boats *(Topic 88)*
A. The floors / or levels on / ships are / called decks / and there are / large windows and / balconies on / upper decks. (8)
B. Some of the / largest / and heaviest / ships are cargo / ships, which take / goods to other / countries to be / bought and / sold. (9)
C. Many of / these transport / products in vast / containers, and food / is kept in / refrigerated / containers to keep / it fresh. (8)
D. Other boats / are much / smaller than / ships. We rely / on fishing / boats to catch / the fish and seafood / we eat, and lifeboats / rescue people / who are in trouble / at sea. (11)
E. Boats are / used for sport / and for leisure / too. There are / rowing boats / on our rivers, yachts / on our lakes / and at sea, and / people on holiday hire / boats to travel / along our canals. (11)

Breakfast and Brunch *(Topic 136)*
A. Hot / drinks such / as tea and / coffee are / drunk at / breakfast, / and cold / drinks, like / orange / juice, are too. (10)
B. There's a / meal between / breakfast and lunch / which is called / brunch. The word / 'brunch' is a combination / of the first two / letters of 'breakfast' / and the last four / letters of 'lunch'. (10)
C. Not everyone / eats brunch. Some / people have brunch / when they get / up too late for / breakfast, so it's / perfect if you've / had a late / night. (9)
D. The food / can be / similar / to breakfast, / or very / different, often / more like / lunch. (8)
E. Ham, / cheese, boiled / eggs, yoghurt, / fruit and bread / are frequently / served as brunch, / and this type of / food is available in / most hotels either / for breakfast or / brunch. (11)

British Politics *(Topic 21)*
A. To do / this, a candidate / has to get / more votes / than any other / candidate in his / or her local / area, which is / called a / constituency. (10)
B. Once / elected, the / new MP / represents all / the people in / his or her / constituency in / Parliament. (8)
C. A party / has to have / a majority of / MPs, or more / than half of the / 650 seats, to win / the election and / become the / government. (9)
D. If no party / manages / to do this, / the parties / with the most / seats try to / gain a small / majority. (8)
E. This is done / by forming a / coalition with / one of the / other parties, so / their combined / number of / seats, or MPs, / is more / than 325. (10)

Care for the Elderly *(Topic 29)*
A. Loneliness / is a / problem / for / many / elderly / people. (7)
B. They feel / lonely / because / they live / alone and / no longer / see, or spend / time with, the / people they / knew when they / were younger. (11)
C. Charities and / councils / try to / help by / arranging for / them to join / groups and take / part in daytime / activities. (9)
D. Much more / could be / done, however, / to deal / with the / situation, including / more regular / visits from / neighbours / and members of / the family. (11)
E. The challenge / for a caring / society is to make / sure elderly / people are / not on their / own, live as / full a life as / possible, and / receive the / care they / need. (12)

Cats and Dogs *(Topic 107)*
A. Cats quite often / jump on / small moving / objects, / especially if / they're / attached / to the end of / a piece of / string. (10)
B. Dogs / like to fetch / objects you've / thrown for / them. They run / after them as / fast as they / can and pick / them up in their / mouths. (10)
C. When / they bring / them back, / some dogs / drop the objects in / front of / you. Others / challenge you / to pull them / out of their / mouths. (11)
D. Dogs are / much / easier to train / than cats. Unlike / cats, they / learn to obey / basic commands. (7)
E. If you / tell a trained / dog to 'sit', it / sits. If you / tell a cat to do / something, / it usually / ignores you. (8)

Charles Dickens *(Topic 13)*
A. Some / of them are / very strange, / others have / amusing names, / and the stories / are about their / relationships and / what happens / to them. (10)
B. There's / love and / rejection, / and married / couples / who are / not suited / to each / other. (9)
C. There are characters / who marry to / improve their social / status, older men / with younger / women, husbands who / are good to their / wives, and others / who are not. (9)
D. Some are kind / and generous, others / are mean or / corrupt. Some / treat children / well and / others are cruel / to them. (8)
E. There / are people who / do bad things in / Dickens' stories, / and many of / his characters have / difficult lives, / but good people / normally find / happiness or / success in the end. (11)

Chemistry *(Topic 47)*
A. Chemists / study chemical / reactions in / substances. They want / to know how / substances react / under different / conditions. (8)
B. They're / interested / in what / happens / when they're / combined or / in contact / with each / other. (9)
C. There are / organic / chemists, who / study carbon and its / compounds, and there / are inorganic chemists, / who study / almost everything / else. (9)

D. The polymer, / petrochemical / and pharmaceutical / industries all / depend / on organic / chemists. (7)
E. There are / millions of organic / compounds, and more / are invented or / discovered every / year, so these / chemists are busy / people! (8)

Children *(Topic 57)*
A. Their / drawings are now / of people with / heads, legs / and arms, and / soon they're / able to draw / a house. (8)
B. When they're / five, they learn / to count using / their fingers, and / they know more / about themselves, / including their / age and their / birthday. (9)
C. They've already / learnt how to / speak, and it's / about this age / that they learn / how to write / a few letters of / the alphabet, and / copy squares / and triangles. (10)
D. Children go / through several / stages of / development, from the / time they're / born to the time / they become / teenagers. (8)
E. At each / stage they develop / quickly, but the / changes that take / place in the early / years, before / they go to / school, are / amazing! (9)

Cities *(Topic 81)*
A. Larger / cities, like / London, have / numerous museums / and art / galleries that / are open / during / the day. (9)
B. These cities / also have / theatres / and cinemas / that you / can go / to in the / evening as / well. (9)
C. There are / plenty of / restaurants / and bars to / choose from / too, serving / food and drink / from early in / the morning / until late at / night. (11)
D. And if you / decide to stay / up late, you / could / go to / one of the / clubs and experience / the nightlife. (8)
E. It / doesn't / matter which / city you / visit or happen / to live / in, there's / always / something to / do! (10)

Climate Change *(Topic 119)*
A. When / we do all / these things, / carbon / dioxide goes / into the air / and causes global / warming. (8)
B. This has / happened / much / more in / the last / hundred years / than it did / in previous / centuries. (9)
C. Our land / and oceans / are getting / warmer. Our / icebergs are / melting and sea / levels are / rising. (8)
D. There's / more very / bad weather / like / heatwaves, / droughts and / storms. (7)
E. There are / more deserts / as well, and / animals and / plants are / dying because / of the changes / in temperature. It's / a serious / global / problem. (11)

Clothes Shopping *(Topic 143)*
A. The shirt / fitted me / perfectly. I / looked in / the mirror / to check / whether it / suited me as / well. (9)
B. I thought / it looked / good on me / so I decided / to buy it, took / it off, and / put my own / one back on. (8)
C. When I / came out of / the changing / room I told / the assistant / that I would / take the / shirt I'd just / tried on. (9)
D. We / went over to / the cash desk / where she took / the shirt and / put it in a / plastic / bag. (8)
E. She asked / me if I would / like to order / some trousers / in my size, so / I did. Then I / paid for my / new shirt, thanked / her for her / help, and left / the shop. (11)

Coaches and Trains *(Topic 94)*
A. Coaches are / usually more / comfortable than / buses. They're / also faster than / buses, partly because / buses tend to / travel within cities / and towns, rather / than between / them. (11)
B. Trains can / be a relaxing / and enjoyable form / of transport, and / it's often quicker / to go by train / than by any other / form of transport, / apart from a plane / or a helicopter! (10)

C. Trains travel / across the / country from the / north to the / south and / the west to / the east. They're made / up of a number / of carriages which / are also called / coaches. (11)
D. Most of the / carriages are for / passengers to sit / in, but there's / usually at least one / buffet carriage where / food and drinks / can be bought, / and on some there / are small restaurants / as well. (11)
E. One disadvantage, though, / is that it can be / very expensive / to travel by / train. Going by road / on a coach or / sharing a car / with friends normally / costs much / less. (10)

Colds and Flu *(Topic 31)*
A. You don't / usually have / to stay in bed / if you have a / cold. Most / people carry / on with their / normal lives even / if they don't / feel very well. (10)
B. If you get / (or catch) flu, / though, you'll / probably feel / much worse and / won't feel able / to study or / work during / the day. (9)
C. With flu, you / could have a / headache or a / fever, which is / when your temperature / rises, or chills, / which is when you / feel very cold. (8)
D. You may / feel hot and / cold at different / times. You'll / also have / some or all / of the cold / symptoms I've / mentioned. (9)
E. Both colds / and flu are / very infectious so / try not to go / near other / people. If you have / flu, the most / sensible thing to / do is to go to / bed and rest / until you feel / better. (12)

Communication *(Topic 55)*
A. We raise a / finger / in front / of our / mouths / when we / want someone / to be / quiet. (9)
B. We clap / and wave with / our hands, point / at something with / a finger, and knock / to let someone / know we're at / the door. (8)

C. In the / UK, if we / point a / thumb / upwards, it / means that / something's / good or it's / gone well. (9)
D. If we / point / it downwards, / it means / it's bad, or / it's gone / badly. (7)
E. A gesture / could have / a different / meaning in / another country, so / be careful / when you use / them abroad! (8)

Computing *(Topic 50)*
A. Inside a computer / there's a plastic / board, called / the motherboard, / which has / the CPU and / the main memory / on it. (8)
B. There's / also a hard / disk drive which / stores all the / data files / and software / applications, and / an optical disk / drive to read / and write / information. (11)
C. Unlike hardware, / software can't / be touched. It's / all the computer / programs that / control the / hardware and operate / the computer. (8)
D. Software is / translated into / codes / which the / hardware can / understand / and process. (7)
E. Hardware / and software / are both / essential to a / computer. One / couldn't / work without / the other. (8)

Continents and Countries *(Topic 111)*
A. Russia / is larger / than / any / other / country / in the / world. (8)
B. Although / about a quarter / of Russian / land is / in the continent / of Europe, the / other three / quarters are in / Asia. (9)
C. To give / you an / idea of how / vast Russia / is, its European / part is the / largest / country in / Europe. (9)
D. The second / largest / country in / Europe is / Ukraine, which / is less than / a fifth / of the / size. (9)
E. After Russia, / the largest / countries on / our planet in / order of their / size or surface / area are Canada, / the US, China, / Brazil, / Australia and / India. (11)

Cooking at Home (Topic 138)
A. Add a / beef stock / cube, a / glass / of red / wine and three / or four / bay leaves / to the mixture. (9)
B. Stir the contents / of the saucepan / carefully / with a wooden / spoon every ten / minutes and cook / the sauce on a / low heat for / at least an / hour. (10)
C. Now take a / chunk of / Parmesan / cheese and / grate it into / a small bowl. Cut / some parsley into / small pieces with / a pair of / scissors and / put it in another / bowl. (12)
D. Boil / a kettle and / pour the water / into a separate / saucepan. Take the / spaghetti from / the packet and cook / it in the boiling / water for about / ten minutes. (10)
E. When / the spaghetti is / soft, separate it / from the water / with a sieve. Now / serve the spaghetti / and the sauce / and sprinkle / the cheese / and parsley / on top. (11)

Crime (Topic 36)
A. Be very / careful with / personal or / financial / information, online / banking and / any passwords / or pin / numbers. (9)
B. Don't buy / drugs from / a drug / dealer. You / can never be / sure what you're / buying and they / could make you / ill or even kill / you. (10)
C. Never get / into a car / with a driver / who's been drinking / alcohol or taking / drugs. You're / much more / likely to be in / a car accident / if you do. (10)
D. If you're / driving, or a / pedestrian, or / a cyclist, look / out for / dangerous / drivers / too. (8)
E. Dangerous / driving is a crime / and people die on / our roads every / day because / motorists / are careless or drive / too fast. (8)

Democracies and Elections (Topic 25)
A. On / polling day, / in each / constituency, / people / go to their / local polling / station to / vote. (9)
B. They are / given / a piece of / paper which / has the names / of the local / candidates / and their parties / on it. (9)
C. They put a / cross next to / the name of / the person / and party they / wish to / vote for. (7)
D. Then they / put their / piece of / paper in a / container / called / a ballot box. (7)
E. At the / end of the / day, all the / votes are / counted and / the candidate with / the most votes / becomes the / member of / parliament for / their local area. (11)

Disability (Topic 28)
A. In 1948 / doctors at a / hospital in the / UK began / using sport / to help / injured / soldiers. (8)
B. Since / then, sport has / been an / important / part of disabled / people's / lives because / of its physical / and psychological / benefits. (10)
C. Millions of / athletes with / disabilities / take / part / in sports / every / day. (8)
D. Many have / competed / in sports / events / like the / Special Olympics, / the Paralympic / Games and the Invictus / Games. (9)
E. Disabled / people in / sport, and in / life, are / showing / the world / what can / be achieved. (8)

Disasters (Topic 118)
A. If there's / a serious / earthquake in / a city or a / large town, / buildings / collapse / and people are / injured and / killed. (10)
B. An / earthquake under / the sea / produces giant / waves which / are called / tsunamis. When / they reach the / coast, people / drown and buildings / are destroyed. (11)
C. There / was a / tsunami in / the Indian / Ocean in December / 2004. Many of / the people who / lived or / were on / holiday next to / the ocean were / killed. (12)

D. After a / disaster there / is sometimes an / epidemic. This can / happen when / serious diseases / spread in disaster / areas. (8)
E. Thousands of / people may / become ill / and die / unless / they receive the / right medical / help. (8)

Diseases in Poor Countries *(Topic 32)*
A. It's common / for people to / have both / malaria / and HIV at / the same / time. (7)
B. When this / happens, their / HIV virus / is much / stronger, so / they infect / other people / more easily. (8)
C. People with / HIV, or who suffer / from malnutrition, can / become ill / with TB. This is / because their immune / systems are / low. (8)
D. In Africa, more / people with / HIV lose / their lives / because / of TB than / anything / else. (8)
E. If there's / malnutrition, dirty / water, and disease / all in one / place, more / men, women and / children are likely to / become sick and / die. It's a tragic / situation. (10)

Diseases in Rich Countries *(Topic 33)*
A. There / are many / types of / cancer, which / affect different / parts of, or / organs in, the / body. (8)
B. Some forms / of the illness / can be / cured, but / people still / die of other / forms unless / they are / diagnosed / early. (10)
C. Other serious / illnesses are heart / disease and / strokes. People / with heart disease / are in danger / of dying / from heart / attacks. (9)
D. If someone has / a stroke, a blood / vessel in / the brain / becomes blocked, or / there's bleeding, and / this can also be / fatal. (8)
E. It's not / all bad / news, though. We're / much less / likely to / die of these / illnesses if we / change our / lifestyles! (9)

Doctors and Chemists *(Topic 34)*
A. If it's a / problem which / is easy to / treat, they / may tell / you to go / back to your / chemist and / buy a cream, / or some / tablets / over the counter. (12)
B. But if you / need a strong / medicine, the / doctor will / give you a / prescription / for it, which is / sent to the / chemist. (9)
C. Once / the medicine / has been / prepared / by the chemist, you / should receive a / text telling / you it's ready / for you to / collect. (10)
D. Your doctor / may not be / sure what / your medical / problem is, in / which case / you would / normally be / referred to see / a specialist. (10)
E. This / means they / arrange for / you to see a / doctor with a / lot of medical / knowledge of the / part of the / body or the / illness that you're / worried about. (11)

Drinks *(Topic 135)*
A. There's sweet / or dry cider / and a choice / of white, red / or rosé / wines. There / are spirits / too, like whisky, / rum and / vodka. (10)
B. Spirits are very / strong, though, / because they / have high / alcoholic / content, so it's / dangerous to drink / too much of / them. (9)
C. Choose a / cocktail / instead. Cocktails / are normally / a mixture / of spirits / and soft / drinks like / fruit juice. (9)
D. Better still, / drink water! / In most / bars and / restaurants you / can ask / for still or / sparkling water / in bottles, or tap / water. (10)
E. To stay / healthy we / need to drink / water every / day. Women are / advised to / drink at least / one and a / half litres a / day, and men as / much as two / litres. (12)

Earning Money *(Topic 128)*
A. The financial / or tax year in / the UK begins / on the 6th / of April in / one year and / ends on the / 5th of April / in the following / year. (10)

B. Inflation is a / word we use / to say how / much the cost / of living goes / up from one month / to the next, so / things online and / in the shops / become more / expensive because / of inflation. (12)
C. In some / jobs people get / a salary or / wages increase / once a year so / they can afford / to buy food and / pay for their / rent, transport and / other costs. (10)
D. If you're / good / at your / job and / you work / hard, you / might get / a promotion / at work. (9)
E. If you do, / you should / get a higher / salary or an / increase in your / wages so you're / earning the / right amount for / your new job. (9)

Earth and Other Planets *(Topic 115)*
A. Life is / only possible / on planets that / have water. A / planet too / close to its / Sun would be / too hot to / have water / on it. (10)
B. Any water / would boil / and turn into / a gas. If a / planet is too / far away / from its / Sun, any / water would / freeze and / become ice. (11)
C. Earth is / the right / distance from / the Sun for life / to exist on / our planet. It's / not too / hot and not / too cold. (9)
D. Although it's / the only planet / we know has / life on it, / it's possible there / are other planets / in other solar / systems where / some forms of / life also exist. (10)
E. Any planet the / same size as / Earth and about / the same / distance from / its Sun could have / the right conditions / for life. (8)

Eating in Restaurants *(Topic 139)*
A. The waiter / serves all / your food / and drink at / your table, unless / there's a buffet, / or it's a fast-food / restaurant, and / you take what / you've chosen to / your table. (11)

B. Once / you've / finished / eating and / are ready / to leave, ask / the waiter / for the / bill. (9)
C. When it's / brought / to your / table you'll / need to / tell the waiter / how you want / to pay. (8)
D. If you're / paying by / debit / or credit card / the waiter will / use a card / machine so / you can make / your payment. (9)
E. Service / is usually / included, but / if it's not, you / may wish / to give / the waiter / a tip for / serving you. (9)

Education *(Topic 60)*
A. The / subjects they / choose / are often / the ones / they did / well in when / they took / their GCSEs. (9)
B. If they get / good enough / grades in their / A levels, they may / be offered / a place on a / course at one of / the country's / universities. (9)
C. After three / or four years / of study, assessment / and exams, students / graduate from / university, which / means they gain / a degree in their / subject. (9)
D. All the hard / work they've / done at / school, at college, / or at university, and / the qualifications they've / gained, are / important. (8)
E. It could all be / a great help to / them, not / only when / they start work, but / in their future / careers as / well. (8)

Education, Health, and Benefits *(Topic 30)*
A. There are also / benefits, which / are payments / provided / by the / government for / people who / need financial / help. (9)
B. For people / who are out of / work and can't / find a job / there's unemployment / benefit. For men / and women / who have / reached retirement / age there's a state / pension. (11)

C. There are / payments / for disabled / people, too, / and for / carers who look / after other / people. (8)
D. Income / support is for / people on low / incomes, and housing / benefit helps / people on / low incomes / to pay their / rent. (9)
E. Many of the / other benefits are / related to / children. There's maternity / benefit, an adoption / payment, and for / families on low / incomes there's child / benefit. (9)

Emergencies *(Topic 37)*
A. After talking / to them, a suspect / may be arrested / if it's believed / a crime has / been committed, or / they disobey / a police / officer. (9)
B. In some / cases, often when / people become / violent, the police put / handcuffs on them / before taking / them to the police / station. (8)
C. At the / police station / someone who's / committed / a serious / offence is normally / charged and / placed / in custody. (9)
D. There are / crimes, however, / that are / considered less / serious, and / in many of these / the offender is / unlikely to reoffend / or cause any / problems. (10)
E. In these / situations, / bail may / be granted, and / the person / released until / they are / due to stand / trial. (9)

Emmeline Pankhurst *(Topic 16)*
A. Although / committed / to direct action / rather than words, / early WSPU / campaigns and / meetings were / mainly peaceful. (8)
B. However, / as they / continued / to be ignored, / the suffragettes / became / more / militant. (8)
C. They / damaged / property, / and met with / opposition / from the / police, which / often became / violent. (9)
D. Many of / them went / on hunger / strikes and / were force-fed / when they / were sent / repeatedly to / prison. (9)
E. Their actions / raised awareness / of the injustice / and inequality / experienced by / women in society / and led to changes / in the law in 1918 / and 1928 which / gave women the / right to vote. (11)

Employment *(Topic 62)*
A. If you are / shortlisted, you'll be / invited to / attend an / interview where / you'll be asked / the same / questions / as other / candidates, or / similar questions. (11)
B. The interview / may be / conducted by the / line manager / of the position / which is vacant, / or by a human / resources / officer responsible / for recruitment, / or both. (11)
C. If you do / well at the / interview you may / be offered the / job, and you'll / be told what / benefits you'll receive / should you decide / to accept. (9)
D. Some / companies / offer training / courses / to new / employees, and / apart from / receiving / a salary, you'll / also get annual / leave. (11)
E. You / will be / able to join a / pension / plan too, which / means / you'll be / given a / pension many / years later / when you / retire. (12)

English Grammar *(Topic 41)*
A. Before students / start their / English course / and attend / their lessons, / they think about / the resources that are / required to / do the course. (9)
B. They may / choose to get / a dictionary and / books on grammar / and vocabulary, / unless they decide / to access / all these resources / online. (9)
C. Students might / not know / what books / to buy or / where to / find the / information they / need online. (8)
D. If this is / the case they / could contact / their teacher, or / the person / who has helped / them register, and / ask for their / advice. (9)

E. People working / at the school / should be able / to advise students / what resources are / recommended or most / suitable for the / course they're / about to start. (9)

English Vocabulary (Topic 42)
A. Of / course, it's / important / to be / able to / pronounce / them / properly. (8)
B. However, we'll / only be able / to add / them to our / vocabulary / when we / learn and / understand what / they mean. (9)
C. English / teachers help / students understand / words by explaining / them in English, and / giving students / vocabulary exercises / to do. (8)
D. A lot of these / exercises are / online and they're / in vocabulary books / too, which students / can use at / home or take / to school. (8)
E. Whenever they / don't know the / meaning of / a word, they / should make / sure they look the / word up online / or use a / dictionary. (9)

Entertainment (Topic 67)
A. Most of / these films / are based / on stories that / were originally / written and published / as novels, biographies, / or other works / of fiction and / non-fiction. (10)
B. Films, current / affairs programmes, / sports / events, drama and / comedy series / are shown on / TV every / day. (8)
C. There's also / a large variety / of other / programmes, / including soap / operas, quiz / shows, and / documentaries. (8)
D. In the / UK in the / 1960s / there were / only three TV / channels: / BBC1, BBC2 / and ITV. (8)
E. Nowadays / there are / hundreds of / channels, so many / in fact, that when / we switch / on the TV, we / often can't / decide what / to watch! (10)

Extreme Weather (Topic 124)
A. As a result, / the US / has every / type of / weather from / droughts to / blizzards. (7)
B. It has more / than a thousand / tornados a year / (or 80% of those / on the planet), / mostly in central / and southeastern / regions, and ten / times as many / thunderstorms. (10)
C. There are also / heatwaves, wildfires, / hurricanes, torrential / rain and / floods which cause / destruction and / loss of life / throughout the / year as they / move across / the country. (11)
D. Europeans / who arrived / in the / US hundreds / of years / ago were / shocked by / the weather they / experienced compared / to weather in / Europe. (11)
E. Although weather / forecasts now / warn Americans / and Canadians of / the dangers, extreme / weather is still / a serious / problem across / the continent. (9)

Finding Accommodation (Topic 76)
A. Estate / agents normally / have the keys / for all their / properties so they / can give / people a guided / tour and show / them what the flat / or house looks / like inside. (11)
B. The owners of / properties are called / landlords or / landladies. They let / properties to / tenants, who are / the people who / rent them. (8)
C. This is / why you / see / signs outside / flats / and houses / which / say 'to let'. (8)
D. Estate agents / also help / people buy / flats and houses, / but property is / expensive, so most / people need to go / to a bank and / get a mortgage. (9)
E. Banks normally / only agree to / give people mortgages / if they have / jobs and earn / enough money to / be able to / afford the / repayments. (9)

Finding Work (Topic 61)
A. It's often / better and / more realistic / to apply for a / temporary / position / or a job / that isn't as / well / paid. (10)

B. By doing this / there's a better / chance of / getting / the opportunity / to work / and gaining / the experience / needed. (9)
C. People / in temporary / jobs can show / their employer / they work / hard, get things / done, and are / an important part / of a team. (9)
D. Some of / them stay / with the / same company / and get a / promotion and / others find / a better paid / or more senior / position / elsewhere. (11)
E. Whatever the / outcome is, the / initial / period / of employment / will usually / have been / very helpful. (8)

Fish and Seafood (Topic 132)
A. Eating / prawns / as scampi / is only one / of many / ways to / enjoy / prawns, though. (8)
B. They're / the most / popular seafood in / both the UK and / the US – where / they're called / shrimps – mainly / because they're / so versatile. (9)
C. Prawns are / delicious in / garlic, with / spaghetti, rice or / noodles, in salads, / soups and curries, / with avocado, and / numerous other / foods. (9)
D. Other / seafood options / include fresh / crab, scallops, / mussels and oysters, / which are / served in / restaurants across / the world. (9)
E. We only eat / them at / home on special / occasions because / they take / time to prepare / and can be / expensive, but / they're much / less expensive / than lobster! (11)

Food from Other Countries (Topic 140)
A. The Germans have / brought us / their sausages – their / frankfurters were / named after / the city of / Frankfurt – and hamburgers / were named / after Hamburg. (9)
B. Pastries, which / can be bought / in most bakers' / and coffee / shops, are / called Danish / pastries because / they were originally / from Denmark. (9)
C. Greek restaurants / serve specialities / like moussaka, / Indian ones offer / curry dishes / with rice, and / the Italians / are famous / all over the / world for their / pizza and pasta. (11)
D. If you go / to a Spanish / restaurant you can / eat some of / their tapas / dishes, and if / you like raw / fish you'll enjoy / Japanese / sushi. (10)
E. There are / too many foods / from around the / world to list them / all here, but if / you spend / time in a city / like London or / Paris, why not try / as many of them / as you can? (11)

Fruit (Topic 134)
A. The next / thing to do / is to slice / some grapes / and strawberries / into two or / three / pieces. (8)
B. To make / the juice, squeeze / the five oranges / that are left into / a large bowl and / add about the / same amount of / water, before / putting all the / fruit in as / well. (11)
C. Raspberries, / pears, and / kiwifruit are / three other / fruit you might / want to / include. Be / careful with / bananas, though. (9)
D. They lose / their colour and / go brown and / mushy if they're / left in the / juice for too / long, so put them / in at the last / minute! (9)
E. Finally, when / you serve / your fruit / salad, why not / add some / yoghurt, and put / a spoonful of / honey on / top? (9)

Furniture (Topic 78)
A. Most of our / furniture is / modern, but a few / years / ago we went / to an antique / shop and / bought some furniture / which is more / than a hundred / years old. (11)
B. The side / table and the / stool we chose / are by / the front / door in the / hall. (7)
C. We put / the antique desk / we bought in / the office, and / the grandfather / clock on the landing / at the top / of the stairs. (8)

D. I don't often / visit antique / shops, but when / I do, I go inside / and see whether / there's anything for / sale that's beautiful / or interesting. (8)
E. If I / think there / is, and I can / afford it, I like / to buy it and / take it / home. (7)

Gambling *(Topic 130)*
A. Gambling a / few pounds / every now / and again can / be fun, but / spending and losing / much larger / amounts of / money causes / serious / problems. (11)
B. For people who / are unable to / control their / gambling, it's a / type of addiction, / like being / addicted to / drugs or / alcohol. (9)
C. The more / money they / lose, the more / desperate they / become to win / it back. When / they run out / of their own / money, they may / steal to carry / on gambling. (11)
D. Apart / from financial / problems, the / addiction can also / result in crime / and destroy / relationships. It / can cause / depression and / anxiety. (10)
E. Help, however, is / available. When gamblers / accept they have / a problem and / decide to do / something about it, / there are organisations / that can help / them to stop. (9)

Gardens *(Topic 79)*
A. Most / people grow / plants and / flowers in their / gardens which / can be put / in the earth / or soil, or / in pots. (9)
B. Some / people also / have a / greenhouse, where / their plants are / protected from / bad weather, and / others have sheds / where gardening / equipment can be / kept or stored. (11)
C. A gardener might / keep a pair / of gardening / gloves, a spade / and a fork in / the shed, as / well as a lawnmower, a / wheelbarrow, and / perhaps even / a hosepipe. (10)
D. Finally, a / patio in / the back garden / is a good / place to put a / table and / chairs. (7)

E. Having a / drink or a / meal there / on a sunny / day can be a / very enjoyable / experience, but in / the UK the weather / isn't always / warm enough for / us to sit outside! (11)

Gears and Pedals *(Topic 92)*
A. When you / press down on / the clutch with / your foot, you can / change gear. This / is difficult / at first but / drivers who / practise it / enough will / find it gets / easier. (12)
B. The pedal / in the / middle is / the brake. This / helps you / slow / down and / stop. (8)
C. To stop / the car / properly you / also need to / put on the / handbrake, especially / if you've parked / on a slope. (8)
D. The pedal on / the right is / the accelerator, which / is used to / increase / or reduce / speed. (7)
E. There are many / other things you / need to learn / about driving, but / once you know / how to use / the pedals and / change gear, everything / else should be / easier! (10)

Geoffrey Chaucer *(Topic 11)*
A. Telling / stories / was a / popular form / of entertainment / in the / 14th / century. (8)
B. In The / Canterbury Tales, a / group of / pilgrims tell / stories to each / other as they / travel together on / a journey from / London to Canterbury / Cathedral. (10)
C. There / are more / than twenty / stories, most / of which were / written in / verse by Chaucer, but / some of / them are / in prose. (10)
D. There's great / variety / in both the story / tellers, who are / in very different / jobs and positions in / society, and in / the stories / themselves. (9)
E. The stories / are interesting, / amusing, and / full of good / and bad / characters, who / do good and / bad things. (8)

George Orwell *(Topic 14)*

A. Written in / 1949, the / book includes / words and terms, / for the first / time, that have / become part / of our language. (8)
B. Big Brother, for / example, is the / dictator who watches / what everyone / is doing, and the / Thought Police use / force to stop / anyone with / opinions different / from those / of the regime. (11)
C. Orwell may / even have / been the first / to use the / expression, The / Cold War, which / described the USA's / and the Soviet / Union's relationship / in the second half / of the 20th / century. (12)
D. These two / novels, which he / wrote not / long before / he died / in 1950, are / easy to / read and very / popular. (9)
E. George Orwell / believed in / using clear and / simple English. One / of his rules / was that a / long word should / never be / used "where a / short one will do". (10)

Giving Directions *(Topic 83)*

A. Keep walking / down the lane, / which bends to / the right, until / you see a pub / and a few / houses on your / left. (8)
B. Go / past / all the / buildings, and / take / the first / left over the / bridge. (8)
C. After about / a hundred / metres / the road / forks. You / need the road that / goes off to the / right. Follow it up / the hill. (9)
D. When / you get / to the farmhouse at / the top, walk / along the / path between / the house and / the field on / your right. (9)
E. You'll see / a sign pointing / to your left / which is / where you'll / find the footpath. It / should take / you about ten / minutes to get / there. Good / luck!" (11)

Growing Up *(Topic 58)*

A. They / choose / their own / vocabulary / and words / to describe / the world they / are in. (8)
B. There are so / many new decisions / to make. Their / parents used to / make most of / these decisions for / them, but not / any longer. (8)
C. They / decide what to / eat and / drink, what / to do in their / free time, / and what games / or sports / to play. (9)
D. They / choose what / clothes to / wear, / what music / to listen to, / and who / to chat with / on the / phone or / Internet. (11)
E. They / decide who / they like, and / when and how / to make / friends. What / they decide to / do makes them / who they are. (9)

Having a Baby *(Topic 56)*

A. When a woman / goes into labour, she / needs to be / taken to / hospital as soon / as possible, unless / she's decided to / have her baby at / home. (9)
B. Most women / choose to / stay in the / maternity / ward of a hospital / for the period / of time, before, / during, and / after the / baby is born. (10)
C. It's reassuring / for them / to know / there are medical / specialists, such / as doctors and / midwives, in / the building. (8)
D. These / places also have / all the medical / equipment needed, and / drugs are / available to help / women who are / in pain. (8)
E. If anything goes / wrong, a hospital / has more / resources to deal / with the / problem, so / it's usually the / safest / place to be. (9)

Henry VIII *(Topic 8)*

A. His fourth / wife was / Anne of Cleves. A / famous painter / called Hans Holbein / showed / Henry / a painting of / Anne. (9)
B. Henry thought / she looked / beautiful in / the painting / and wanted to / meet her, / but was / disappointed / when they / actually met. (10)

C. Although / they got / married, / they didn't / stay together / because he had / already decided / he preferred / a seventeen-year-old / girl called Catherine / Howard. (11)
D. Catherine became / his fifth wife, but / before long / she was also / accused of / having sex with / another man, and / she suffered / the same fate / as Anne Boleyn. (10)
E. Henry's / sixth and / last / wife, Catherine / Parr, lived / longer / than he / did. She was / lucky. (9)

Hobbies *(Topic 69)*
A. Some / of us enjoy making / things, too, like / clothes, jewellery / and models, and / collecting coins / and stamps. (7)
B. A number / of pastimes / usually take / place outdoors / because being / outdoors is an / important or / necessary part of / the activity. (9)
C. Gardening / and metal / detecting, for / example, as well / as camping, fishing / and flying / kites, are / all outdoor / activities. (9)
D. Walking, sailing, / and golf are all / sports, but they're / hobbies too, and / are normally outdoor / activities for the / same reasons. (7)
E. Most other / sports, though, / can be / played either / outside, or / inside at a / leisure or sports / centre. (8)

Holidays *(Topic 89)*
A. Some people / prefer skiing / holidays to / beach holidays. Skiing / holidays are / in the winter / months, and one / of the most / popular places / to ski in Europe / is the Alps. (11)
B. These are / mountains that / cover a / huge area in / eight different / countries, including / Austria, Switzerland, / Germany, France and / Italy. (9)
C. People / who go / skiing also hope / to have good / weather, and / good snow for / skiing is / important. (8)
D. Skiers / take warm / clothes with / them on / holiday / because it / can be very / cold on / the slopes. (9)
E. When they / arrive at their / ski resort they / normally hire / everything else / they need, including / skis, sticks, boots, / helmets and / goggles. (9)

Hospitals *(Topic 35)*
A. Hospitals have / a number / of departments / for different / types / of injury or / sickness, such / as burns and / cuts, cancer and / heart disease. (10)
B. There's / normally a maternity / department as / well, and for / very serious / injuries / or illnesses there's / an intensive care / unit. (9)
C. Most / departments have / rooms called / wards and there / are beds in / each ward for / inpatients. (7)
D. People who / have medical / insurance may have / a private / bedroom and can / normally choose / to go to a / private / hospital. (9)
E. In the / UK, however, / most large / hospitals are / part of the / NHS, or National / Health Service, and / are public / hospitals. (9)

Houses *(Topic 77)*
A. On the / ground / floor most / houses have / a sitting / room and a / kitchen. (7)
B. There may / be a separate / utility room, / dining / room and possibly / a downstairs bathroom / or toilet. (7)
C. If anyone / living / in the house / works from / home there / could also / be an office. (7)
D. In most / houses the bedrooms / and bathrooms are / upstairs on the / first or second / floors and there's / a flight of / stairs that you / go up to / reach them. (10)
E. Some elderly / people who / find walking / difficult live in / bungalows, which / don't have / any stairs. (7)

How Animals Look (Topic 102)
A. Mammals like / dogs and / cats tend to / be less / colourful, with / fur that's / usually black, / white, brown, grey, / ginger or yellow. (9)
B. One / that's extremely / colourful, though, is / the male / mandrill, / which is / a large / monkey. (8)
C. Charles / Darwin, / the naturalist / and biologist, / believed it / was the most / colourful / mammal in / the world. (9)
D. It has dark / green or grey / fur and its / bottom / is bright / pink and / blue. (7)
E. It also / has a / long, red nose, / a bright / blue face, / and a yellow or / orange beard! (7)

How Animals Move (Topic 103)
A. Frogs / and toads / hop and / jump, / and so do / insects like / grasshoppers, and / mammals like / kangaroos. (9)
B. Most / animals with / four / legs can / run, and / some, like / cheetahs / and lions, can / run at great / speed. (10)
C. Horses / run very / quickly as / well, but we / normally say / they gallop / rather than / run. (8)
D. Of / course, human / beings / only have / two / legs, and / we can / run too. (8)
E. There's / a large / bird with / two legs, / though, that / can run / much / faster than we / can. It's called / an ostrich! (10)

How Animals Sound (Topic 104)
A. Wild / animals in / Africa and / other / continents / also / make / sounds. (8)
B. People / who go / on safaris / hear these / animals during / the day, but / some of / the sounds they / make at night / are amazing. (10)
C. Birds sing, / whistle, tweet / and twitter. / Monkeys / chatter / and lions / roar. (7)
D. Elephants / trumpet, wolves / and wild dogs / howl, frogs / croak and snakes / hiss. Even insects / make sounds. Bees / and flies buzz. (8)
E. In hot / countries one / of the loudest / noises at / night is the / sound of crickets / chirping and we / often hear / mosquitos whine / before they / bite us! (11)

Howard Carter (Topic 4)
A. When they / opened the / door / and entered / the room, they / found / priceless gold and / ebony / treasures. (9)
B. At one / end of the / room there / was a sealed / door, with two / statues / of soldiers / guarding it. (8)
C. This / door led / to another / room where / they found / the tomb of / Tutankhamun. (7)
D. It was almost / intact, and the / room contained / hundreds of / objects, many / of them covered / in gold, or painted / in beautiful / colours. (9)
E. They had / been placed / there because / it was / believed the young / pharaoh would / need all his / possessions in / the afterlife. (9)

How We Look (Topic 52)
A. When / people get / older, their / hair normally / goes / grey, and in / many cases / turns white. (8)
B. There's / a wide variety / of different hairstyles / as well, and / the choice of a / centre parting, a / side parting or / a fringe. (8)
C. For / people / with long / hair, a / ponytail, bun or / plaits are / options. (7)
D. Finally, although / a lot of / men shave / every / day, others / grow stubble, / or have / a beard or a / moustache. (9)
E. With so / many / possibilities, no / wonder / we all / look / different! (7)

How We Move (Topic 53)
A. We stretch / our arms / and legs when / we get / up in the / morning, or before / exercise, and we / often fold our / arms, or cross / our legs. (10)

B. We turn our / heads and / shrug our / shoulders. We / wave with a / hand and point / with a finger. (7)
C. We lean / forwards, backwards / or against a / wall, bend our / knees, pick something / up, put it / down, carry it / somewhere, throw / it or catch it. (9)
D. Sometimes / our bodies / move / when / we don't / even want / them / to. (8)
E. We tremble / with fear, shiver / with cold, and / jump when someone / or something / gives us / a shock! (7)

How We Sound *(Topic 54)*
A. We whisper / to say something / quietly, / shout to say / something loudly, / and scream because / we're furious, / terrified or in / agony. (9)
B. The voice / does other / things too. It's / used as a musical / instrument, not only / to sing, but / also to hum / and whistle. (8)
C. We intend / to make these / sounds, but there / are other sounds / we don't normally / make on / purpose. (7)
D. Anyone with / a cold might / sneeze or / cough, babies / burp, and / we sometimes / hiccup again and / again until we / drink some / water. (10)
E. There's one / sound, though, that / we're almost always / unaware of. When we're / asleep some of us / snore so loudly / we wake other / people up! (8)

How We Think *(Topic 51)*
A. We have / feelings and / memories, and / think / about time, / life and / death, / and right / and wrong. (9)
B. Our / use of / language has / enabled us / to communicate / and understand / each / other. (8)
C. We / have / personality, / humour, and self-control, / and / appreciate beauty / and pleasure. (7)
D. With / these extraordinary / developments, human / beings have / become / the most / advanced and / powerful / creatures on / the planet. (10)
E. With / power, though, comes / responsibility. All / of us, and in / particular our / governments, have / a responsibility / to protect / life, the environment / and the world / we live in. (11)

Insects *(Topic 109)*
A. Wasps like / to fly around / us too. They / can be / irritating, and / if they / sting you, / it's painful. (8)
B. Some / insects, like / locusts, cause / problems for / farmers because / they damage / their crops. This / is why farmers / use pesticides to / control and kill / them. (11)
C. Other / insects, called / moths, damage / our clothes. Put / some mothballs / in your drawers / and wardrobes / and they'll stay / away. (9)
D. Not all insects / are a problem, / though, and / some are / wonderful. Butterflies / have wings that / are beautiful / colours. (8)
E. Bees / provide us / with honey, / and silkworms, a / type of moth, / produce silk / which is used / to make ties, / shirts and / dresses. (10)

Interviews *(Topic 63)*
A. What else / can you tell / them that will / encourage them / to offer / you the / position? What / questions will / you ask at / the end? (10)
B. Your appearance / is important / too. Spend / time deciding / what to / wear, so / it's right for / the job, the / company and / the occasion. (10)
C. Start your / journey early / so you're / not in / a hurry, and / are calm and / ready when / you arrive / at reception. (9)

D. Employers / don't like / people to be / late for / work, so they / won't be / happy if you're / late for your / appointment! (9)
E. Finally, during / the interview, listen / carefully, be / relaxed, be confident, / and answer the / questions in a / positive and / enthusiastic / way. (9)

Isaac Newton *(Topic 2)*
A. In fact, he / soon realised / it could explain / how all the / objects in the / universe are / affected by / the force, which / became known / as gravity. (10)
B. Newton's / discovery was / followed / by his three / laws of / motion, / which were / published / in a book / twenty / years later. (11)
C. He is also / famous for his / work on light, / what it does, / and how / white light is / composed / of all the / colours of the / rainbow. (10)
D. He invented a / telescope that / used mirrors to / reflect light, / and calculus, / which is / a type of maths / to do with / rates of change. (9)
E. None / of these great / achievements, / though, are as / well-known / as the story / about the apple, / and how it / helped Newton / discover gravity. (10)

JK Rowling *(Topic 15)*
A. Harry Potter / uses his magical / powers to / defend himself / and others / against evil / wizards, and his / main enemy, Lord / Voldemort, who / killed his parents / and wants to / kill him. (12)
B. The novels and / the eight / films based / on them are / full of wonderful / stories / and characters. (7)
C. Children / and adults / all over / the world have / enjoyed them / since the first / book was / published / in 1997. (9)
D. JK Rowling / went on / to write / novels for / adults using / the pen / name Robert / Galbraith. (8)
E. She is best / known, however, / for her Harry / Potter novels / which have / sold more / copies than any / other book / series. (9)

Jobs *(Topic 65)*
A. Many of our / students are / working as / au pairs, cleaners, / waiters and / baristas, but these / are temporary / jobs while they're / in the UK. (9)
B. What they / would really like / to do as a / career, and / the jobs some / of them are / doing now, are / very different. (8)
C. I asked / my students to / think about the / question / for a few / minutes, before / talking to each / other about the / occupations that / interested / them. (11)
D. These are some / of the careers / they were interested / in: interior / designer, engineer, IT / specialist, accountant, / farmer, estate / agent, chef, architect, / receptionist, journalist, and / dentist. (10)
E. They're / all jobs that / people can hope / to get and be / successful / in, provided they / have the right / qualifications, skills, / and experience. (9)

Kitchen Things *(Topic 75)*
A. When we / take crockery / out of the / dishwasher, it's / all put away / in two cupboards, / or on long / shelves between / the cupboards. (9)
B. We keep / our mugs / and cups in one / of the cupboards, and / glasses for / water, wine / and soft / drinks in the / other. (9)
C. Plates, / bowls and / saucers are / arranged / on one / of the / shelves. (7)
D. Below the / shelves there's / a worktop, which is / the surface we / prepare most / of our food on, / and drawers / containing all / our kitchen / utensils and / cutlery. (11)
E. Under the drawers / there's a large / cupboard which has / our saucepans, a frying / pan and a baking / tray in / it. Whatever / it is, there's / a place for it / in our kitchen! (10)

Languages *(Topic 113)*

A. The language / with the third / largest number / of native speakers in / the world is / English. It's the / main language in the / UK, the US, / Canada, Ireland, / Australia and New / Zealand. (11)

B. After English / comes Hindi, which / is the most / common first / language in India, / a country with the / largest population in / the world. (8)

C. Arabic is / next, with about / 300 million / native speakers, / most of whom / are in North / Africa and / the Middle / East. (9)

D. Portuguese / is also / spoken as / a first / language by / a large / number of / people. (8)

E. Did you / know there / are far / more native / speakers of / Portuguese in / Brazil than in / Portugal? (8)

Learning to Drive *(Topic 91)*

A. There are / many other / things you / need to / learn as / well, and one / of the most / important is the / expression "mirror, / signal, manoeuvre". (10)

B. Before you / drive around / a roundabout, or / turn left or / right into / another road / you should always / look in your / mirrors first. (9)

C. Then / you indicate, or / signal, with your / indicator so other / drivers and / pedestrians know / what you're / about to do. (8)

D. Finally, you / manoeuvre, which / means you change / your speed, your / direction or your / position. If this / sounds difficult, don't / worry! (8)

E. Your driving / instructor will / teach everything / you need to / know, and you'll / be able to / practise it again / and again until / you drive well / enough, and safely / enough, to pass / your test. (12)

Leonardo da Vinci *(Topic 1)*

A. He designed / contact / lenses, a type / of calculator, / and a clock that / was more / accurate / than any other / at the time. (9)

B. He may / even have / discovered what / hurricanes and / other types / of weather look / like, and / how they / move. (9)

C. He / understood that / air, although / invisible, / moved in the / same way / as water when / there was a / hurricane. (9)

D. No-one / else was / able to / see this / until satellites / gave us / pictures of the / weather about / 500 years / later. (10)

E. Leonardo / da Vinci, / who was / born / in 1452 and / died in / 1519, / was a / genius. (9)

Life and Death *(Topic 150)*

A. Governments have / a responsibility / to make sure / people in need / receive proper / care, especially when / they become ill / or frail in old / age. (9)

B. People who are / suffering or in / pain can now be / given better medical / treatment and drugs / than at any time / in history, so their / experience is less / painful and / difficult. (10)

C. With advances / in medical / science, a priority / this century should / be to make / dying as painless as / possible for those / who are near / the end of / life. (10)

D. When someone / dies, we should / remember / they are at / peace, before, / during, and / after the / funeral. (8)

E. Finally, if / it's their / wish, let's / throw their / ashes into / the wind, in / a place they / once loved. (8)

Local Government *(Topic 27)*

A. The services / that are / provided by / local government / include education, / transport, leisure, / housing, waste and / social services. (8)

B. Social / services departments / are responsible / for the care and / support of disabled / and elderly / people, as well / as children / and adults at / risk. (10)

C. There are / other services / provided / by councils / too, such as / parking, roads, / libraries, the emergency / services and / planning. (9)
D. Planning / departments deal / with applications, for / example, to / replace a / door or a / window, build / an extension, or / change a building / into flats. (10)
E. The National / Health / Service, or NHS, / is not provided / by local / councils, but / almost everything / else is. (8)

Looking after Children (Topic 98)
A. Medicines and / household or garden / chemicals should / be kept away / from children to / prevent babies / or small children / swallowing them or / burning their / skin. (10)
B. Gardening / equipment, like / lawnmowers, and sharp / tools should / also be stored / out of children's / reach, locked / in a garden / shed if you / have one. (10)
C. Make / sure / children are / a safe distance / away from / any equipment / when it's being / used. (8)
D. Whenever / there's a / barbecue, / a bonfire, / or fireworks, / keep children / well away. (7)
E. If you're / walking on / the pavement, however, / or across or near / a road, hold small / children's hands / and keep them / as close to / you as possible. (9)

Lunch, Tea, and Supper (Topic 137)
A. This / is very different / from lunch in / a restaurant, or / Sunday lunch at / home, which / takes a lot / longer. (8)
B. Tea is usually / a light meal / which people / have in the / afternoon, / either at / home, or in / a tearoom, hotel / or restaurant. (9)
C. It might / just be a / pot or a cup / of tea, but / biscuits, scones, / cake, and even / sandwiches, are / often part / of afternoon / tea as well. (10)
D. The words used / for meals, / though, can be / confusing. Different / words are / used in the / north of / England and / other parts / of the country. (10)
E. For example, tea / in many family / homes in the / UK is an early / supper, especially for / children, rather / than a cup / of tea in / the afternoon. (9)

Martin Luther King (Topic 18)
A. It also / led to / changes / in US / law which / ended legal / segregation. (7)
B. In 1964, aged / 35, he / became the / youngest / man to / win the Nobel / Prize for / Peace. (8)
C. Despite / this, his life / was often in / danger, and in / 1968 he was / assassinated / by a gunman in / Memphis, / Tennessee. (9)
D. In the / US, the third / Monday every / January is / a national / holiday in his / honour. (7)
E. Schools, public / buildings / and more / than 700 streets / in cities and / towns have / been named / after him. (8)

Maths (Topic 49)
A. Other types / of maths are / taught in schools / and universities, such / as algebra, geometry, / statistics, probability / and calculus. (7)
B. In algebra, letters / and symbols are / used to represent / quantities, whereas / geometry is to / do with the measurements / and relationships of lines, / angles, surfaces / and solids. (9)
C. Statistics is all / about information / shown in numbers / which give us / a better idea / of what is / happening in / a particular / situation. (9)
D. Probability, often / expressed in / percentages, is / about the future / and the chances / that something / will happen. (7)

E. Calculus deals / with rates of / change, for / instance, in a / population over / a period of / time, or the speed / of a moving object / from the start / to the end of / its movement. (11)

Matilda *(Topic 6)*
A. When it was / dark, dressed in / white and / accompanied / by a number / of knights, she / was lowered / down the / castle walls. (9)
B. Once / she reached / the snow-covered / ground, she crossed / the frozen River / Isis and walked / straight past her / cousin's army to / safety. (9)
C. Although / Matilda controlled / much of the / southwest / of the country / while Stephen / was king, / she never / became queen / of England. (10)
D. However, when / her cousin / died in / 1154, he was / succeeded / by Matilda's eldest / son, who became / King Henry II. (8)
E. Matilda / returned to / Normandy in / 1148, where she / worked with / the Church and founded / monasteries. She died / in 1167 and is / buried in Rouen / Cathedral. (10)

Meat *(Topic 131)*
A. I've been / buying vegetarian / sausages for a / while now, but / more recently / I've started eating / a wide variety / of other / foods that no / longer contain / meat. (11)
B. I've / realised for / the first / time in my / life that I / could, and / probably should, / become a / vegetarian. (9)
C. I'm concerned / about animal / welfare and, as / I get older, I'm / more concerned / about my own / health, and what's / good for me. (8)
D. Vegetarian and / vegan food is / now widely / available in supermarkets / and shops, and it / tastes so much / better than it / used to years / ago. (9)
E. There are plenty / of reasons / why it makes / sense to stop / eating meat, and / it's never been / easier to / do. (8)

Medical Emergencies *(Topic 96)*
A. In less serious / situations where it / isn't an emergency / but someone doesn't / feel very well / or has had a minor / accident, call 111. (7)
B. You may be / able to give / the person first / aid, especially if / you've been on / a first aid training / course. (7)
C. Even if you / haven't been / trained, there / are first aid kits / and guides to basic / first aid that / could help you / deal with the / problem. (9)
D. If you've / got one / of these / guides, you / should / be able / to help / with an / insect bite / or a sting. (10)
E. A bruise, a minor / burn, or a cut / can be treated as / well, as can a / minor sports / injury, but if you / think it's a broken / bone, get medical / help. (9)

Michael Faraday *(Topic 3)*
A. In 1831 / Faraday / discovered / in another / experiment that / he was able / to reverse the / process, and / turn mechanical / energy into / electrical energy. (11)
B. He had / created the / dynamo, the / very first type / of generator, / a machine / that produces / electricity. (8)
C. Modern generators / now convert / fossil fuels, / nuclear power / and renewable / energy into / the electricity we / use every / day. (9)
D. Michael / Faraday / discovered / some of the / most / important / laws of / chemistry and / physics. (9)
E. His / inventions / of the electric / motor and / the generator / were two / of the greatest / in history. (8)

Money and Currencies *(Topic 126)*
A. While the / euro is the / most common / currency in / Europe, the / dollar and / the peso are / also used in / a large number / of countries. (10)
B. In North / America, the US / and Canada have / the dollar, and / it's used in / numerous other / countries as well, / including Australia / and New Zealand. (9)

C. In South / America, Argentina, / Chile, Colombia / and Uruguay all / have the / peso as / their currency. (7)
D. And in other / continents, China / has the yuan, / Japan has / the yen, Russia / the rouble / and South / Africa / the rand. (9)
E. In total, / there are / about 180 / different currencies / in the world, / almost as / many as there / are countries. (8)

Music *(Topic 68)*
A. A few of the / best and most / talented / musicians, who / play their / musical instruments / or sing in / front of audiences, / eventually become / famous and wealthy. (10)
B. Successful / musicians tended / to have a / recording contract / and go to a / studio to record / their songs, and / these were / played on the / radio and on TV. (10)
C. Times have / changed, / though. Nowadays / music can be / downloaded and much / of it is listened / to on a desktop / or laptop / computer. (9)
D. Most / people / only / play / musical / instruments as / a pastime. (7)
E. They / play music on / their own, or / for their family / and friends, usually / because it's / fun and they / enjoy it. (8)

Numbers and Calculations *(Topic 44)*
A. For years such / as those in / the first decade / of the century, we / tend to say two / thousand and / one up to / two thousand / and nine. (9)
B. After that, though, it's / common for us / to say the first / two numbers and / then the second two / numbers, so twenty / ten and twenty / eleven, right up to / twenty ninety-nine. (9)
C. If we were to / write the years / I've mentioned in / this paragraph as / numbers, we / would write 2001, / 2009, 2010, 2011 / and 2099. No / commas are / used for years / written as numbers. (11)
D. Calculators / on mobile / phones / make it / easier to do / calculations / anywhere / and any time. (8)
E. In the / English language we / use the words 'plus, / minus, times / and divided / by' for each of / the main types of / calculation. (8)

Oceans *(Topic 112)*
A. The largest / ocean is / the Pacific, which / is west / of North / and South / America, and / east of Asia / and Australia. (9)
B. It is so / large that its / surface area / is greater / than all the / land in the / world put / together. (8)
C. The / second largest / is the Atlantic / Ocean which / is between / the Americas, / and Europe and / Africa. (8)
D. After the / Atlantic, the / other oceans, in / order of their / size, are the / Indian Ocean, / the Southern Ocean / and the Arctic / Ocean. (9)
E. The Arctic Ocean / is not only / the smallest / ocean, it's also / the most / northern and / the shallowest. (7)

Pedestrians and Cyclists *(Topic 100)*
A. Cyclists / are much / safer if / they wear / helmets and / keep a safe / distance between / themselves and / all other / vehicles. (10)
B. It's / dangerous for / them to / overtake / on the / inside of / other / vehicles. (8)
C. In the / UK, some / of the worst / accidents happen / when they try / to cycle past / lorries or / cars which are / about to turn / left, and don't / see them. (11)
D. They should / always use lights / when it's / dark or / there's poor / visibility, and / wear brightly / coloured clothing / that helps / drivers see / them during / the day. (12)
E. Finally, they / must / do what / traffic lights / and signs / tell them / to do. Going / through a red / light can cause / a serious / accident. (11)

People at Work *(Topic 64)*

A. Employees / report / to a manager, / who in larger / companies is / accountable to / a more senior / manager, who / might be a / managing / director. (11)

B. Companies / usually have at / least one / person whose / job is in / sales, another / in marketing, and / someone in a / financial / position, often a / qualified accountant. (11)

C. Other / employees deal / with human / resources, or / HR, public / relations, or / PR, and / information / technology, / or IT. (10)

D. There's / normally / a customer / services person / or team as / well, to help / resolve any / problems. (8)

E. By employing / people / with different / skills, knowledge / and experience, / companies are / usually well / placed to deal / with most work / issues and / everyday / tasks. (12)

Physics *(Topic 48)*

A. We rely / on electromagnetic / energy every time / we switch on / a light, or turn / it off. There's / even energy stored / in stretched or / squashed objects. (9)

B. Waves are / also sources of / energy. They're / used in many / different / ways, and our / ocean waves / generate a / vast amount / of energy. (10)

C. They're / used for TV / and radio signals, / microwave / ovens and mobile / phones, and / for X-rays / and radiotherapy in / hospitals. (9)

D. Of course, / light waves / also make / it possible for / us to see. Sunlight / is a mixture of / electromagnetic / waves, or radiation, / from the sun. (9)

E. Physics / is extraordinary. It / explains much of / what happens on / Earth, and answers / many questions / about the universe / as well. (8)

Places to Visit in London *(Topic 85)*

A. The capital / city has numerous / historic / buildings too, such / as the Houses of / Parliament, the Tower / of London, St Paul's / Cathedral / and Buckingham / Palace. (10)

B. If you like / art, and in / particular, paintings, go / to Trafalgar / Square where you'll / find the National / Gallery, and the / National Portrait Gallery, which / is nearby. (9)

C. There's so much / to see in the / museums that a visit / to the British Museum / or the Science Museum / would be a great / idea. (7)

D. There are / also some unusual / buildings to see / from the / outside such / as the London / Eye, the Shard and / the Elizabeth / Tower. (9)

E. You can visit / all of these / places by / taking the / Tube, but going on / a boat cruise on / the River Thames, or / an open top bus / tour through the / streets of the / city, would be / more fun! (12)

Planes and Flying *(Topic 86)*

A. The passengers / put / on their / seatbelts again / when the / journey is almost / over. (7)

B. The plane then / flies down / towards the / land. When / this happens we / say the plane / is landing. (7)

C. Once it's on / the ground / again, it moves / slowly along the / runway until / it gets / to the airport. (7)

D. Soon after it / stops, the captain / thanks everyone / for choosing / to fly with the / airline and wishes / them a pleasant / stay in the city or / country they've just / arrived in. (10)

E. The passengers / then undo their / seatbelts, take / their hand / luggage, get / off the / plane and walk / into the airport. (8)

Plants *(Topic 110)*
A. We wouldn't / have drinks / like tea or / coffee without / plants, and we / get a lot of / our medicines from / plants, including / aspirin. (9)
B. Many of the / products we buy / in shops come / from plants. Anything / made of / plastic or / rubber, for / example. (8)
C. Soap, shampoo, / paint and all / our clothes made / from cotton are / also from / plants, and what / about the wood / we get from / trees? (9)
D. Wood is / used to make / buildings and / boats, furniture / and fences, paper / and cardboard, as / well as thousands / of other things. (8)
E. Trees and / other plants / are so useful / and important / that we couldn't / live without / them. (7)

Poverty and Hunger *(Topic 117)*
A. The worst / disasters / happen, / though, during / a period of / weather with no / rain, which / is called a / drought. (9)
B. When / there's / a drought / there's often / little or / no water or / food. (7)
C. People / who are very / thirsty may / drink dirty / water which causes / disease. Without / food or water, they / lose weight, become / ill and are desperate / for help. (10)
D. They are so / hungry that they / starve. International / organisations provide / aid as soon / as they can, but / much more could / be done to / help these people / and save their / lives. (11)
E. There / are still / millions of / men, women / and children / who try to / survive every / day without clean / water or enough / to eat. (10)

Preventing Burglaries *(Topic 99)*
A. If you're going / away for / a holiday or some / other reason, don't / tell anyone you / don't know / well, and / never leave this / information on / an answering / machine. (11)
B. Burglars often / find out / people's / numbers / and call / them to see / if they're at / home. (8)
C. A fence / can help prevent / a burglar from / getting into / your back garden, / but it needs to / be high enough / for them to have / trouble climbing / over it. (10)
D. Put locks / on the doors / of garden sheds / and garages as / well, because valuable / objects worth / hundreds / of pounds, and / cars worth thousands, / are kept / there. (11)
E. Being part / of a neighbourhood / watch scheme / can also help, / as can a dog. A / burglar can't / be sure whether / a dog will / bite them, but / they wouldn't normally / take a / chance! (12)

Public Transport *(Topic 93)*
A. Three / of the / busiest / and most famous / are the / Northern / line, the District / line and the / Central line. (9)
B. The stations / and many of / the lines are / actually above / the ground. Escalators, / lifts and stairs move / people from one / level to another / so they can catch / a train to work / or to go home. (11)
C. Buses also / cross the city in / every direction. In / London many of / them are red and / have two levels, a / lower deck / and an upper / one, where people / can enjoy views / of the city. (11)
D. They take / longer to / reach their / destination because / of the traffic, but / are a good / way to travel / unless you're in / a hurry. (9)
E. There / are cars, and / bikes, that people / can hire / too, and there's / even public / transport on the / river, so they / can travel by / boat. (10)

Punishment and Prison *(Topic 40)*
A. Another / punishment / for less / serious / crimes is / community / service. (7)

B. Community service / is unpaid / work which is / done in the local / area to help / local people. The / judge in court / decides how / long the / community / service / should be. (12)
C. There are / more people in / prison in the / UK than at any / time in the / past, and / about 95% / of them are / men. (9)
D. Many of / these prisoners / are behind bars / either for / a long / time or a / very short / time. (8)
E. About / 20% of prisoners / are serving a / life / sentence, but / almost 50% / are in / prison for six / months or / less. (10)

Richard III *(Topic 7)*
A. The young / princes were / never seen / in public / again. Their / disappearance / and their uncle's / actions made / people think / he had arranged / their murder. (11)
B. Richard and / a distant cousin / called Henry Tudor / were both / descended / from King / Edward III, who / had died more than / a century / earlier in / 1377. (11)
C. Henry also / believed he / had a right / to be king. In / August / 1485 he led / an army / against Richard / and won / the Battle of / Bosworth Field. (11)
D. Richard was / killed in the / battle and for / hundreds of / years no-one / knew where / he was / buried. (8)
E. In 2012 a / skeleton was / found under / a car park / in the city / of Leicester. Experts / examined it very / carefully and a DNA / test confirmed that / it was Richard's. (10)

Safaris, Zoos, and Farms *(Topic 106)*
A. For most / of us, the / only / places we / see wild / animals are on / TV or in / a zoo. (8)
B. Animals in zoos / are kept in / cages or / enclosures so / they can't / escape, often / in conditions / which people / consider cruel. (9)
C. Other animals are / kept on farms, / and for hundreds / of years these / farms have / provided us / with much of / what we want / or need / in our daily lives. (10)
D. We get / our dairy / products from / cows and / goats, our eggs / from hens, and / our wool from / sheep. Beef, pork, / chicken and / lamb all come / from farms. (11)
E. While animal / welfare is / still a serious / issue for farm / animals, organic / farming has begun / to make a real / difference in the / UK. (9)

Safety at Home *(Topic 97)*
A. Keep / clothes, furniture / and curtains / away from / all heating / appliances, such / as cookers. (7)
B. Be very / careful with / candles, cigarettes, / lighters and / matches. An / adult should / always be in / the room when / they're lit and / put out. (10)
C. Finally, never / touch electrical / appliances / with wet / hands or / take one / into the / bathroom. (8)
D. Water / conducts / electricity, / and being / electrocuted / could kill / someone. (7)
E. Your / home should / be the / safest / place in the / world. Make / sure it is. (8)

Safety on the Roads *(Topic 95)*
A. If there's a / serious accident / anywhere in the / UK, call 999 as soon / as possible. The / emergency services / arrive at the / scene as soon / as they can get / there. (10)
B. They're able / to arrive / at most / accidents quite / quickly, / even when / there's a lot of / traffic on the / roads. (9)
C. This is / not only because / their vehicles are / driven at high / speed, but / also because / of their sirens / and flashing / lights. (9)
D. When other / people in / cars hear / a siren or see / flashing lights in / their mirrors, they / try to move over / to the side of the / road so an ambulance, a / police car or a fire / engine can go / past them. (12)

E. The emergency / services save / thousands / of lives every / year when they / drive across / our towns and / countryside to / help people / who have / been in an / accident. (12)

Samuel Pepys *(Topic 9)*
A. He / went to the / Tower of / London to get / a good view / and then / decided to take / a boat onto / the River / Thames. (10)
B. From the / river he could / see houses / burning and people / desperately trying / to remove / possessions from / their homes. (8)
C. Pepys / wrote in / his diary that he / went to tell the / king as soon / as he realised / how serious the / situation was. (8)
D. It's not / known how / many people / died in the / disaster, but / more than / 13,000 / houses were / burnt down. (9)
E. Many / of London's / historic / buildings were / also damaged / or destroyed in / the fire, / including St. / Paul's Cathedral. (9)

Shapes and Sizes *(Topic 45)*
A. Clothes / are small, / medium, large or / extra-large, / and the same / adjectives are / used for eggs in / supermarkets, except / the largest / are 'very large'. (10)
B. We also / use numbers for / clothes, including / measurements for / the collar, chest, / waist and / legs, and sizes / for dresses, socks / and shoes. (9)
C. In the / UK, the capital / letter A is / used with a / number for / files, envelopes / and pieces / of paper. (8)
D. Once you / know it's A3 / for the large / ones, A4 for / medium-sized / ones, and A5 / for smaller ones, / you'll get the / right size. (9)
E. Whenever you / look for something / online, or in a / shop, there are / usually words, letters / or numbers, or a / combination of / these, to help / you find what / you want. (10)

Shopping Online *(Topic 145)*
A. Customers, / though, can / have a very / different / experience / when they / shop / online. (8)
B. If you read / about a / company and the / reviews warn you / about awful / service or / terrible products, / that's probably / what you'll / get. (10)
C. They may / get back to / you quickly / if you want / to buy / a product, but / don't waste / any time / or money on / companies with / bad reviews. (11)
D. Many of them / are very difficult, / if not impossible / to reach when / you try to / contact them about / a problem with / a product you've / already bought. (9)
E. If you're / still unsure about / a company after / reading their / reviews, why not / send them an / email or a / text, or call / them, to see how / they respond? (10)

Shops *(Topic 142)*
A. You can get / your medicines or / anything you want / to keep in your / bathroom from your / local chemist's, and / the estate / agents on the / high street will / help you / find a / property. (12)
B. If you / need just one or / two everyday / items, the convenience / store on the / corner of / your street / is the place / to go. (9)
C. There / used / to be / a shop / for almost / everything, / but not / anymore. (8)
D. Online / shopping / and companies / that deliver / anything you / need to your / home have / changed the / way shopping is / done. (10)
E. Shops are / closing down / every / day, especially / in our high / streets, because / they can't / make any / money. (9)

Sightseeing and Tourism *(Topic 90)*
A. Take photos / of the buildings / and the squares, / the statues and / the fountains. Walk / through one / of the parks or go / on a tour of / the city. (9)

B. In the / evening you can / stay in your apartment / or your hotel / if you're / tired, or go / out and enjoy / the nightlife if / you're not! (9)
C. Try some / of the local / food and / drink. In big / cities, there's / a choice of hundreds / of restaurants, bars / and nightclubs. (8)
D. You / could go / to the / cinema / to see a / film, or / the theatre / to watch / a play. (9)
E. If you / like / music, go / to a / concert. Whatever / you do, have / a great / time! (8)

Spending Money *(Topic 129)*
A. Be careful, / though. If you / forget, or don't / have enough / money to pay / your credit card / bill, you'll pay a / large amount / of interest to / the bank. (10)
B. If you choose a / debit card instead, / you'll only be / able to spend what / you have in your / account, or up / to the maximum / of an overdraft / allowance agreed / with your bank. (10)
C. You may / find it easier / to control / your spending / with a debit / card than / a credit / card. (8)
D. Try to stay / in credit if you / can. If you / owe your / bank money, you / may be / offered a / loan to pay / back what / you owe. (10)
E. Like being / overdrawn, / though, you'll / have to / pay a lot of / interest to the / bank, so it / could be / expensive. (9)

Sports and Places *(Topic 70)*
A. If you go / to watch / these sports / played by / professionals, the / venue would / normally be / a stadium with / a pitch inside / the stadium. (10)
B. There / are different / venues, though, / for other / sports. Horse / racing takes / place at a / racecourse / and golf is / played on / a golf / course. (12)
C. We can / watch athletics / at an athletics / track, motor / racing at a race / track, and / cycling at a / cycling track or in / a building called / a velodrome. (10)
D. We swim and play / water polo / in swimming / pools, some / with diving boards / at one end, and / there are pools in / sports and leisure / centres. (9)
E. Whatever / we want / to do, there's / usually / somewhere / we can / do it! (7)

Sports Equipment *(Topic 71)*
A. The helmet is / used to protect / your head / and the / pads / are used to / protect your / legs. (8)
B. There / are eleven / players in a / team, / and one / of the players / is called / a wicket keeper. (8)
C. The wicket / keeper stands / behind a piece / of equipment / called a / wicket, / which is / made / of wood. (9)
D. He, or / she, is the / only player / in the team / who needs / two pairs / of gloves. (7)
E. One / pair is / to bat with, / and a much / larger pair / is to / keep / wicket with! (8)

Stephen Hawking *(Topic 20)*
A. Stephen Hawking, / who was / born in / 1942 and / died in / 2018, / was a physicist, / author and / researcher. (9)
B. He is best / known / for his / work on the / origins and / development / of the / universe. (8)
C. He suffered / from a serious / illness for most of / his life, but in / spite of this / he continued to / work as a / cosmologist, and / a spokesperson and role / model for / disabled / people. (12)
D. He and / eleven others / signed a / charter on disability in / 2000 which demanded / human and civil / rights for the world's / 600 million / disabled people. (9)
E. He was / involved / in many fundraising / activities and gave / numerous talks, / lectures and / interviews on / disability. (8)

Supermarkets *(Topic 144)*
A. Pasta, cereals, / biscuits and tea / are mostly in / packets, and much / of this food is / likely to be / on shelves in / one or two of / the aisles. (9)
B. Drinks are all / in the same / location as / well, with bottles / and cans of soft / drinks near / alcoholic / ones, like / beer, wine / and spirits. (10)
C. You can / buy almost / anything in / a supermarket. If / there's something / you need for / your family, dog or / cat, your kitchen / or your bathroom, / you'll find / it there. (11)
D. There's always / a lot of fresh / food, but plenty / of frozen food as / well. Supermarket / freezers are / usually full of / frozen vegetables, / meat, fish, and / ice cream. (10)
E. Make sure, / though, you / put it in your / trolley just / before you go / to pay. If you / do, it should / still be frozen / when you get / home! (10)

The Animal Family *(Topic 101)*
A. They / may have / gone their / separate ways 50 / million / years / ago, but seals / and dogs are / related too. (9)
B. Female / mammals give / birth to / their babies / and feed / them with / their milk. (7)
C. This / makes them / different / from birds, / and reptiles / such as crocodiles, / snakes / and tortoises, / all of which / lay eggs. (10)
D. Mammals / are also / different / from birds / because, / with one / exception, they / can't fly. (8)
E. Can you / think of a / mammal that / has wings and / can fly? / The answer / to the question is / bats, the / only flying / mammals on / Earth! (11)

The Arts *(Topic 66)*
A. The theatre / is where / plays are / performed, which / is why / theatre is often / known as a / performing art. (8)
B. Cinema, / opera, ballet, / dance and / music concerts are / also called / performing / arts, because / in all of / these, the artists / or performers perform / in front of / an audience. (12)
C. Music is / featured in / almost all the / performances. Classical / music is a very / important part / of opera, ballet and / some concerts, and / it's used in plays / and films as / well. (11)
D. There are / many other / types of / music, though, / which are / played in public / performances, but / are also enjoyed / by people at / home. (10)
E. When / we listen to / music, when we / sing, dance, or play / a musical / instrument, we experience / an art form / which, in one / form or another, is / available to / everyone. (11)

The Body *(Topic 148)*
A. Below / the chest / is the / stomach, / which / is above / the waist. (7)
B. Below the waist / on each / side are / our hips, which are / just above / the bottom, / which is / below the back. (9)
C. Below / the bottom / we have / two legs, / which / bend at / our knees. (7)
D. At the / end of the / legs are two / feet, and in / between each leg / and each foot / there's a part of / the body called / the ankle. (9)
E. Each foot / has five / toes. This / ends our / journey / from / head to / toe! (8)

The Countryside *(Topic 82)*
A. Most / countryside is / inland, but / it extends to / the coast as / well, next / to the sea. (7)
B. There / are areas of / still water / that are right / in the middle / of the / countryside, such / as lakes and / ponds. (9)
C. There's moving / water, too. / Streams / descend / from hills or / mountains / and become / rivers, and rivers / eventually flow / into the sea. (10)

D. Life in the / countryside / is usually / quieter, more / peaceful and / more relaxed / than in the / cities. (8)
E. It's a / good / place to / retire for / older people / who no longer / work. (7)

The Courts *(Topic 39)*
A. One of / the barristers / defends the / accused by / arguing they / haven't committed / a crime and / are therefore / innocent. (9)
B. The / other barrister / prosecutes / the accused by / arguing they have / committed a / crime and are / guilty. (8)
C. When the / jury have / considered / what they've / heard, they make / their decision, which / is called / reaching / a verdict. (9)
D. If they / conclude / they're guilty, the / accused is / convicted / and the judge / announces / what punishment is / to be given. (9)
E. If the jury / believe they're / innocent, the accused / is acquitted, and / the judge states / officially in court / that they can / go free. (8)

The Environment *(Topic 120)*
A. Food is / transported / thousands / of miles, which / causes / pollution / and wastes / resources. (8)
B. We could / buy / food that's / produced / nearby, or / has come from / the farm down / the road. (8)
C. Think of all / the things we / no longer use / or need. Clothes, / books and / some of those / old things in / the attic can / go to a / recycling bank or / a charity shop. (11)
D. Why / do we have / to drive to / work every / day when we / could leave our / cars at home and / take public / transport instead? (9)
E. These are / all ways we / can stop / wasting things, / and help to / protect the / environment. Let's / see how many / ideas we can / put into / action. (11)

The European Union *(Topic 23)*
A. Most / EU countries / have the same / currency, the / euro, although / some countries / use their own / currency. (8)
B. The European / Central Bank in / Frankfurt, / Germany, has / policies for the / euro, and in / particular, / keeping inflation / under control. (9)
C. This means / making / sure the price / of everything / in the shops / doesn't / go up too / quickly. (8)
D. The UK joined / the EU in / 1973. On / the 23rd of June / 2016, after 43 years / of membership, a / referendum was / held to decide / whether the UK / should remain / in the EU. (11)
E. 52% of people / who voted chose / to leave, and 48% / to remain. In a / process that / came to be / known as / Brexit, the UK / ceased to be / a member of / the EU. (11)

The Family *(Topic 149)*
A. My mother / and father are / standing beside / them, and my mother's / parents (my grandmother / and grandfather), / are also at the / front, next to / my father. (9)
B. My aunt, uncle, / older brother, and / my nephew / and niece, are / all in the / background, in / the row behind. (7)
C. My / cousin, who's / the same / age as / I am, is / standing / just in front / of my uncle. (8)
D. All the members / of the groom's family / are on the / other side of the / newly-wed couple. I know / who they are / now, but I didn't / on the day of / the wedding. (9)
E. I'd met my / brother-in-law / on several occasions, / but the first / time I met other / members of his / family was at / the reception. (8)

The Forecast *(Topic 125)*
A. Tuesday will / bring more / showers, mostly / in the west, but / elsewhere it / should be / a relatively dry / day. (8)

B. It will / feel very / cold in the / wind, which is / likely to get / stronger later / on, especially in / the afternoon. (8)
C. The outlook / for Wednesday, / Thursday and / Friday is much / improved / with rising / temperatures and / only a chance / of isolated / showers. (10)
D. It will feel / milder, with / daytime temperatures / as high / as eleven or / twelve Celsius, / although the / nights will be / cold. (9)
E. It's expected / to be drier / than the first / half of the / week, with less / rain, but the possibility / of snow showers / on higher ground in / the north of England / and Scotland. (10)

The Four Seasons *(Topic 123)*
A. Some autumns / the weather / stays warm / during the / day until / October, and / even the / nights are / mild. This is / known as an / Indian Summer. (11)
B. December, / January and / February are / winter / months. Winter/ is the / coldest, wettest / and windiest / season. (9)
C. Towards the / end of winter / there is usually / less wind and / rain, but it / becomes even / colder and it / often snows. (8)
D. It also begins / with the shortest / days of the / year. In London / on the 21st / of December, sunrise / is just after / 8am and sunset is / just before / 4pm. (10)
E. It's usually / the / shortest / day of / all with / about eight / hours of / daylight. (8)

The History of Shopping *(Topic 141)*
A. The / first shops / with windows / which / displayed / goods were / in London in / the late / 18th / century. (10)
B. Shop owners / realised they / needed to / attract customers, so / they used / advertisements and / arranged everything / they wanted to / sell in their / shop windows. (10)
C. In the / 19th century / the first department / stores were / opened with / a wide / range of / items in / different departments. (9)
D. Later / on, shopping / centres were / built indoors so / customers could / walk from one / shop to another / in the same / building. (9)
E. Some shopping / centres are / in cities and / towns, but others / can be / found outside / urban areas. (7)

The Industrial Revolution *(Topic 10)*
A. Steam engines, for / example, replaced / water and horse / power in many different / industries. For this / reason, factories could / be built anywhere / for the first / time. (9)
B. It became / much easier and / faster to produce / textiles, iron, / steel and / coal, which / led to a huge / increase in / production. (9)
C. New and / better ways / of farming were / also introduced / and between / 1700 and 1850 / production on / farms almost / doubled. (9)
D. As a result / of these / changes Britain / became / a great / trading / nation. (8)
E. There / were important / changes in / education / too. A number / of laws in / the 1800s made / education available / and free to / all children. (10)

The Police *(Topic 38)*
A. Another / responsibility / for the / police is / to respond / to calls / from the / public / about crimes / and accidents. (10)
B. They / speak to, and / support, the / victims of / crime and / witnesses, collecting / evidence and / taking / statements. (9)
C. They / also carry / out investigations / using the latest / technology or traditional / methods. Part / of an investigation may / be to search / people, property, / vehicles or land. (10)

D. It's not / all exciting / detective work, / though, because / they have to / do a lot of / administration as / well. (8)
E. When they / get back / to the police / station / all the / information / has to be / recorded and / put in a / report. (10)

The Seaside *(Topic 84)*
A. It's a lovely / temperature on a / warm day in / summer, refreshing / but not cold, so / people enjoy / going in to / swim, and playing / games / in the water. (10)
B. On the / beach there's a / café that serves / sandwiches, ice / creams and cold / drinks, and a hut / nearby where the / lifeguards work. (8)
C. They / watch what / everyone's / doing to / make / sure we're all / safe and no-one's / in any danger / in the water. (9)
D. Next to / the sandy / area in front / of the hut, / and to the / left, are some / rocks / and a number / of rockpools. (9)
E. Children go / there with nets / and buckets to / catch shrimps, which / are like small / prawns, and tiny / crabs. (7)

The Welfare State *(Topic 26)*
A. The welfare / state in the / UK was created / between 1906 / and 1914, when / there were / reforms to help / young and elderly / people who / were poor. (10)
B. Free school / meals and / medicals were / given to / children, and / there was / financial support / for adults who / were sick, or / too old to / work. (11)
C. This was / followed, years / later in 1942, / by the Beveridge / report, named / after William / Beveridge, an / economist / and social / reformer. (10)
D. The report / advised the / government to / provide enough / income, health / care, education, / housing and / employment for / people in / need. (10)
E. By 1948 new / laws had been / introduced which / resulted / in the practical and / financial help / the Beveridge report / had asked / for. (9)

Tools *(Topic 72)*
A. People / enjoy looking / for objects / made / of metal / wherever / they think / they might be, / including fields, / beaches, gardens / and parks. (11)
B. Most metal / objects in / the ground, like / bottle / tops and / nails, aren't / of any real / interest. (8)
C. When / something old, /unusual or / valuable is / discovered, though, / it can be very / exciting for the / person who / finds it. (9)
D. Metal / detectors / can / detect / objects / made / of gold, silver / and / bronze. (9)
E. They've / often been / used to find / jewellery such / as rings, / earrings and / coins, some / of which are / hundreds of / years old! (10)

UK Political Parties *(Topic 22)*
A. In particular, they / said they would / create jobs, / halve violent / crime, reform the / health service / and education system, and / cut household / bills by using / cheaper electricity. (10)
B. In recent / decades, there / have been three / parties – after the / Conservatives and / Labour – that have / won more seats / in the House of / Commons than / the others. (10)
C. These are the / Liberal Democrats, / the SNP, or Scottish / Nationalist / Party and the / DUP, or Democratic / Unionist Party / of Northern / Ireland. (9)
D. In 2010 the / Conservatives asked / the Liberal Democrats, / and in 2017 they / asked the DUP, to / join them in / order to form / a coalition / government. (9)
E. The Conservatives / needed their MPs / to gain a small / majority / of seats in the / House of Commons / and become / the government. (8)

Vegetables *(Topic 133)*
A. Vegetables go / well with other / foods too. Have / you tried / chicken with carrots / and sprouts, or fish / with new / potatoes and / peas? (9)

B. Another dish / I would / recommend is / steak in a peppercorn / sauce with mushrooms / and spinach, / and cauliflower and / cheese are / such a good / combination there's a / dish called cauliflower / cheese! (12)
C. What about / green beans and / broccoli? They're tasty / as part of almost / any cooked dish / served hot, but / they're enjoyable / cold as well, especially / in salads on / a warm day. (10)
D. In the / winter, though, / when it's / cold, why / not use the / vegetables in / your fridge or / larder to make / a hot vegetable / soup? (10)
E. There are / hundreds of / different / ways of / eating / vegetables. Just / ask a / vegetarian! (8)

Wars *(Topic 116)*
A. In the two / World Wars, / more than a / hundred million / people were / killed, wounded / or died, and more / than half of / them were / civilians. (10)
B. Wars between / countries and / civil wars have / continued in / the 21st / century, but / there is some / hope that a third / World War will / not happen and / we can live in / peace. (12)
C. Before / nuclear / weapons, governments / and military / leaders / believed they / could win / a war. (8)
D. With nuclear / weapons, / countries / at war are / likely to / destroy each / other. (7)
E. The dangers / are so / great that / a war with / these weapons / is not an / option. (7)

What Men Wear *(Topic 147)*
A. Over these clothes / they usually wear / a shirt above / the waist, and / trousers below it, / but when it's / hot, or when / they're playing / sports, a lot of / men wear shorts. (10)

B. Businessmen / used to / wear a formal / shirt and a / tie, but nowadays / most men who / are at work prefer / to undo the / top button of / their shirt / instead. (11)
C. Many of them / wear a / jacket over / the shirt, or / a suit, which / is a jacket / and matching / trousers. (8)
D. When / men are at / home they / wear more / casual clothes, / and a lot / of young / men wear / jeans, a T-shirt / and trainers. (10)
E. Older men usually / wear socks / and shoes on their / feet. Most shoes are / black or brown, / but they can be / any colour. Some / shoes have laces / and others don't. (9)

What Weather! *(Topic 122)*
A. When it's / cold and raining / outside, and / we're sitting / in a warm / room at / home, we tell / each other / how cosy it / feels. (10)
B. We / can't resist / talking about / unusual weather / either. Storms are / exciting, so when / we hear / thunder or see / lightning we can't / wait to tell / someone. (11)
C. Snow's exciting / too, especially when / it's going to / snow / heavily, so we / let each / other know. (7)
D. We love to / predict the / weather and tell / people what the / forecast has / predicted, so we / do that as / well. (8)
E. In / fact, we enjoy / talking about / the weather so / much it's often / the first thing / we mention! (7)

What Women Wear *(Topic 146)*
A. In winter, they / may also wear a / sweater, and put / on a coat, a hat / and a scarf when / they go out. On / their feet they / wear shoes or / boots, and gloves / on their hands to / keep them warm. (11)
B. More women / than men wear / jewellery. They / wear necklaces / and earrings, rings / on their / fingers, and / bracelets on their / wrists. (9)

C. Women also / wear make-up, and / we use the / same verbs to / describe how / it's worn as the / verbs that are / used for wearing / clothes. (9)
D. Women put / make-up on in / the morning, wear / it during the / day or in / the evening / and then take / it off. (8)
E. There are / many different / types of / make-up, but / two of the / most popular / are lipstick / and mascara. (8)

William Shakespeare *(Topic 12)*
A. Shakespeare's histories / are mostly / about English / kings called / Henry and / Richard, who / ruled between / the 13th and / 16th centuries, / and a civil war / known as the / Wars of the Roses. (12)
B. He / also / wrote Roman / plays about / Coriolanus, Julius / Caesar, and Antony / and / Cleopatra. (8)
C. All of these / plays were / based on the / lives of real / people in history, and / many are tragedies, / very sad / stories with / unhappy endings, as / well as histories. (10)
D. This is because / the main / characters find / themselves in bad / situations or do things / which cause them / to lose everything / they have, including / their lives. (9)
E. Romeo / and Juliet, / Hamlet, and King / Lear, are all / main characters / in three of / Shakespeare's / best-known / tragedies. (9)

Winston Churchill *(Topic 17)*
A. During the / summer of 1940, / however, he / made a number / of speeches in / the House of Commons / which won him / the support and / respect of / politicians / of all parties. (11)
B. The British / public, and millions / in the US and across / the world, were / also deeply / affected by his / radio / broadcasts. (8)
C. They gave / people belief and / hope that Britain / would defend / itself against / Adolf Hitler / at a very / dangerous and / difficult time. (9)
D. When he / spoke, he repeated a / number of words to / great effect, none / more so than 'victory' / (winning the war), / and 'fight' / (taking action to stop / the enemy). (9)
E. Churchill's / speeches / inspired / a nation, and / encouraged its / armed / forces to carry / on fighting until / the Second World War / ended / in 1945. (11)

Words for Feelings *(Topic 43)*
A. He'd been / offered a job / he really wanted, / but he / seemed so / surprised. I asked / him why / it was surprising. (8)
B. He / explained / that something / embarrassing / happened at the / interview, which / made / him feel very / embarrassed. (9)
C. Someone / brought him / a cup of / tea and / he knocked it / over. The / tea went / all over the / table, the floor / and the wall. (10)
D. He was so / disappointed. He'd / convinced / himself / he wouldn't get / the job, / which was / terribly disappointing / for him. (9)
E. When he / told me what / happened, though, I / couldn't stop / laughing. I was / very amused / because the / story was so / amusing! (9)

Words for Weather *(Topic 121)*
A. In the / UK we don't / have extreme / enough weather / to experience / serious hurricanes / or tornados, but / we do have gales / and strong / winds. (10)
B. Windy weather / is usually / unpleasant, but / a gentle / breeze, especially / on a hot / day, can be / refreshing and / pleasant. (9)

C. The words / we use for rain / are to do with / how much rain / there is. When / it's been / raining but / it's stopped, we say / it's wet or it / feels damp. (10)
D. Light / rain / is frequently / called drizzle / and a short / period / of rain is / a shower. (8)
E. Heavy rain can / be described as / a downpour, and / some of us use / the expressions 'it's pouring / with rain', and 'it's / raining cats / and dogs'! (8)

Work and School *(Topic 73)*
A. My laptop, / printer, / phone and a / calendar are / all on my / desk. On one side / of the desk there's / a cupboard that / has all my / files in it. (10)
B. On the other / side, I keep a / small bin to / put rubbish in, / and larger ones / for paper, / cardboard, and / anything / else that can / be recycled. (10)
C. Outside my / office / there's a / corridor which / leads to other / offices and a / meeting / room. (8)
D. The meeting / room, which is at / the end of / the corridor, / has a large, round / table in it, a / whiteboard on / the wall, a flip / chart in one / corner, and a coffee / machine in another. (11)
E. When / we have / meetings, we / usually start / with a cup / of coffee, before we / talk about the / work we're / doing, and / try to make / decisions! (11)

World Records *(Topic 105)*
A. The / fastest / creature / in the / world / is a bird / called a / peregrine / falcon. (9)
B. These / birds have / been / known to fly / faster than 320 / kilometres per / hour, or 200 mph, / which stands / for 'miles per / hour'. (10)
C. The fastest / land animals / are cheetahs, which / can run at a / speed of more / than 96 kph, / or 60 mph, and / some of the / slowest are / tortoises. (10)
D. These / very slow / animals, though, / have also / lived the / longest. In 1770 a / British explorer / called Captain Cook / gave a tortoise / to the Tongan / royal family. (11)
E. It was alive / in three / centuries / and died in / 1965 at the age / of at least / 188. It was one / of the oldest / animals that has / ever lived. (10)

World Religions *(Topic 114)*
A. Hinduism, the / third largest / religion, is / practised / mainly in / India, and has / many different / Gods. (8)
B. Buddhists believe / in a teacher / called / Buddha, but not / in God. Most / Buddhists live in East / Asia and South / East Asia. (8)
C. They practise / meditation in / silence by / focusing on / one thing, / clearing the mind / of other thoughts, / and becoming / very calm. (9)
D. In the / three main / religions, / believers normally / pray to / God / instead. (7)
E. There are / also people who / don't believe / in God, who are / called atheists, and / people who don't / know if God / exists, who / are called / agnostics. (10)

INDEX OF TOPICS

A	(Page)
Adults	118
Airports	174
Alexander Fleming	10
American Politics	48
An Evening In	160

B	
Bank Accounts	254
Barbara Jordan	38
Bathroom Things	148
Biology	92
Birds	216
Boats	176
Breakfast and Brunch	272
British Politics	42

C	
Care for the Elderly	58
Cats and Dogs	214
Charles Dickens	26
Chemistry	94
Children	114
Cities	162
Climate Change	238
Clothes Shopping	286
Coaches and Trains	188
Colds and Flu	62
Communication	110
Computing	100
Continents and Countries	222
Cooking at Home	276
Crime	72

D	
Democracies and Elections	50
Disability	56
Disasters	236
Diseases in Poor Countries	64
Diseases in Rich Countries	66

Doctors and Chemists	68
Drinks	270

E	
Earning Money	256
Earth and Other Planets	230
Eating in Restaurants	278
Education	120
Education, Health, and Benefits	60
Emergencies	74
Emmeline Pankhurst	32
Employment	124
English Grammar	82
English Vocabulary	84
Entertainment	134
Extreme Weather	248

F	
Finding Accommodation	152
Finding Work	122
Fish and Seafood	264
Food from Other Countries	280
Fruit	268
Furniture	156

G	
Gambling	260
Gardens	158
Gears and Pedals	184
Geoffrey Chaucer	22
George Orwell	28
Giving Directions	166
Growing Up	116

H	
Having a Baby	112
Henry VIII	16
Hobbies	138
Holidays	178
Hospitals	70

INDEX OF TOPICS

Houses	154
How Animals Look	204
How Animals Move	206
How Animals Sound	208
How We Look	104
How We Move	106
How We Sound	108
How We Think	102
Howard Carter	8

I
Insects	218
Interviews	126
Isaac Newton	4

J
JK Rowling	30
Jobs	130

K
Kitchen Things	150

L
Languages	226
Learning to Drive	182
Leonardo da Vinci	2
Life and Death	300
Local Government	54
Looking after Children	196
Lunch, Tea, and Supper	274
Martin Luther King	36

M
Maths	98
Matilda	12
Meat	262
Medical Emergencies	192
Michael Faraday	6
Money and Currencies	252
Music	136

N
Numbers and Calculations	88

O
Oceans	224

P
Pedestrians and Cyclists	200
People at Work	128
Physics	96
Places to Visit in London	170
Planes and Flying	172
Plants	220
Poverty and Hunger	234
Preventing Burglaries	198
Public Transport	186
Punishment and Prison	80

R
Richard III	14

S
Safaris, Zoos, and Farms	212
Safety at Home	194
Safety on the Roads	190
Samuel Pepys	18
Shapes and Sizes	90
Shopping Online	290
Shops	284
Sightseeing and Tourism	180
Spending Money	258
Sports and Places	140
Sports Equipment	142
Stephen Hawking	40
Supermarkets	288

T
The Animal Family	202
The Arts	132
The Body	296
The Countryside	164
The Courts	78
The Environment	240
The European Union	46
The Family	298
The Forecast	250
The Four Seasons	246
The History of Shopping	282
The Industrial Revolution	20
The Police	76
The Seaside	168
The Welfare State	52
Tools	144

U
UK Political Parties	44

V
Vegetables	266

W

Wars	232
What Men Wear	294
What Weather!	244
What Women Wear	292
William Shakespeare	24
Winston Churchill	34
Words for Feelings	86
Words for Weather	242
Work and School	146
World Records	210
World Religions	228

www.ingramcontent.com/pod-product-compliance
Ingram Content Group UK Ltd.
Pitfield, Milton Keynes, MK11 3LW, UK
UKHW050627050625
6249UKWH00023B/665